Guid

VOL 22 / PART 1

Edited by **Jeremy Duff and Katharine Dell**

Suggestions for using *Guidelines*

Set aside a regular time and place, if possible, when you can read and pray undisturbed. Before you begin, take time to be still and, if you find it helpful, use the BRF prayer.

In *Guidelines*, the introductory section provides context for the passages or themes to be studied, while the units of comment can be used daily, weekly, or whatever best fits your timetable. You will need a Bible (more than one if you want to compare different translations) as Bible passages are not included. At the end of each week is a 'Guidelines' section, offering further thoughts about, or practical application of what you have been studying.

You may find it helpful to keep a journal to record your thoughts about your study, or to note items for prayer. Another way of using *Guidelines* is to meet with others to discuss the material, either regularly or occasionally.

Occasionally, you may read something in *Guidelines* that you find particularly challenging, even uncomfortable. This is inevitable in a series of notes which draws on a wide spectrum of contributors, and doesn't believe in ducking difficult issues. Indeed, we believe that *Guidelines* readers much prefer thought-provoking material to a bland diet that only confirms what they already think.

If you do disagree with a contributor, you may find it helpful to go through these three steps. First, think about why you feel uncomfortable. Perhaps this is an idea that is new to you, or you are not happy at the way something has been expressed. Or there may be something more substantial—you may feel that the writer is guilty of sweeping generalization, factual error, theological or ethical misjudgment. Second, pray that God would use this disagreement to teach you more about his word and about yourself. Third, think about what you will do as a result of the disagreement. You might resolve to find out more about the issue, or write to the contributor or the editors of *Guidelines*. After all, we aim to be 'doers of the word', not just people who hold opinions about it.

Writers in this issue

Eryl W. Davies is Reader and Head of the Department of Theology and Religious Studies at the University of Wales, Bangor. He gained his doctorate from the University of Cambridge. He is the author of a commentary on the book of Numbers and a volume on feminist criticism of the Old Testament, entitled *The Dissenting Reader*.

Jeremy Frost is Precentor and Liturgist at Canterbury Cathedral. He read music and theology at Oxford University, and was curate of a large church in Wellington, Shropshire. He has recently completed a Masters course in Systematic Theology at King's College, London, focusing on the theological relationship between Israel and the Church.

Alec Gilmore is a Baptist minister, writer and lecturer on biblical themes. He was formerly editor of Lutterworth Press and is the author of *A Dictionary of the English Bible and its Origins* (Continuum).

Christopher Byworth is now officially retired after a ministry combining pastoral ministry in several dioceses in the Church of England with New Testament study and teaching, including a period as Warden of Cranmer Hall in Durham. He continues to teach and serve.

Adrian Curtis is Senior Lecturer in Hebrew Bible at the University of Manchester. He is a Methodist layperson. His writings include a study guide to the book of Joshua and a commentary on the book of Psalms.

Dick France is recently retired from a lifetime of Christian ministry. Most recently he was Rector of seven small parishes on the Welsh border. He is the author of many books, including two commentaries on Mark (the *International Greek Testament Commentary* and BRF's *People's Bible Commentary*) and a further book, *Divine Government: God's Kingship in the Gospel of Mark* (1990).

Jeremy Duff is Director of Lifelong Learning in Liverpool Diocese and Canon at Liverpool Cathedral.

Further BRF reading for this issue

For more in-depth coverage of some of the passages in these
Bible reading notes, we recommend the following titles:

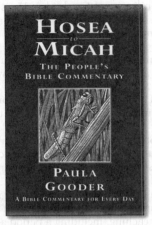

HOSEA to MICAH

THE PEOPLE'S
BIBLE COMMENTARY

PAULA
GOODER

A BIBLE COMMENTARY FOR EVERY DAY

1 84101 245 9, £8.99

JOSHUA and JUDGES

THE PEOPLE'S
BIBLE COMMENTARY

STEVEN D.
MATHEWSON

A BIBLE COMMENTARY FOR EVERY DAY

1 84101 095 2, £7.99

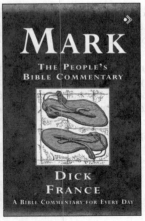

MARK

THE PEOPLE'S
BIBLE COMMENTARY

DICK
FRANCE

A BIBLE COMMENTARY FOR EVERY DAY

1 84101 046 4, £8.99

The Editors write...

In this issue we take a look at the book of Numbers—after Leviticus, the most neglected in *Guidelines*, but brought to life for us by Eryl Davies from the University of Wales at Bangor. We continue our theme of different characters in the Old Testament, featuring Joshua, who famously fought the battle of Jericho but did much else besides, as Adrian Curtis from Manchester University makes clear.

We also continue our coverage of the minor prophets and once again, Alec Gilmore, who has written for us a number of times before, guides us through—this time the short but powerful book of Amos. Amos challenged the opulent people of his day to cease their corruption and has been an inspiration through the centuries for those standing up for social justice in the face of oppression. Here we explore the themes in this passionate prophetic book that was addressed to the eighth century BC but still contains many resonances for us today.

Within the New Testament we study two of the more difficult books—first, Paul's second letter to the Corinthians. This sometimes dense and confusing letter contains great truth and honesty about the reality of life and Christian ministry with its troubles and conflicts: we are ably guided by Christopher Byworth, bringing together his lifetime of experience in pastoral ministry as well as academic expertise. Second, Jeremy Duff, our New Testament editor, invites us to travel to explore the rather alien land of the book of Revelation, which, just like Amos, is a passionate prophetic book with much to say to us today, however much it is often misused. We approach Easter in the company of Dick France, concluding his series on Mark's Gospel. Like Jesus' disciples, we accompany Jesus to his death in Jerusalem and receive, as his original disciples did, the news of his resurrection and the promise that he will meet us again.

As we listen to God's word, it is right that we turn to worship. Jeremy Frost from Canterbury Cathedral leads us in two weeks' reflection on worship, as an activity not just of prayer, praise and penitence but one that encompasses our whole lives. We hope that this edition of *Guidelines* will assist you in your life of worship, discipleship and service.

Katharine Dell, Jeremy Duff

The BRF Prayer

Almighty God,
you have taught us that your word is a lamp for our
feet and a light for our path. Help us, and all who
prayerfully read your word, to deepen our
fellowship with each other through your love. And
in so doing may we come to know you more fully,
love you more truly, and follow more faithfully in
the steps of your son Jesus Christ, who lives and
reigns with you and the Holy Spirit,
one God for evermore. Amen.

NUMBERS 10:11—20:13

The book of Numbers can probably boast the dubious distinction of being one of the least-read and least-studied books in the entire Bible. In some respects, this is hardly surprising, for its very title appears off-putting. The title is rather misleading, however, for the numbers and numerical lists that it contains (such as the census of the Israelite tribes in 1:20–47; 26:5–51) constitute only a relatively small portion of the book as a whole. In fact, it was the Greek translators who gave the book the title 'Numbers' (Greek: *Arithmoi*), and, since Jerome adopted this as the name of the book in the Latin Vulgate (*Numeri*), the title was adopted for the book in all subsequent English translations. In the Hebrew version, however, the book has a different title—'In the wilderness'—and there is a sense in which this is a far more accurate reflection of the nature of its contents, for the primary concern of the book is with the years spent by the Israelite tribes 'in the wilderness' as they journeyed from Mount Sinai to the promised land.

The book of Numbers is frequently divided, for convenience, into three sections. The first section (1:1—10:10) records the events that took place while the Israelites were encamped at Sinai during the second month of the second year after they had come from Egypt. The second main division of the book (10:11—20:13) covers the events that occurred in the vicinity of Kadesh, where the bulk of the 40 years in the wilderness were spent. The final part of the book (20:14—36:13) contains a miscellaneous collection of narratives and laws, most of which are represented as having taken place, or having been formulated, during Israel's stay at Moab.

Our readings will cover the second main division of the book, beginning at 10:11. This section is dominated by the theme of Israel's persistent disobedience and rebellion, which provoke God's anger and lead to the postponement of entry into the promised land until all the rebellious generation have died. Since some of the chapters in this section do not provide a continuous and unified account, it will sometimes be necessary to take verses out of sequence so that the thread of the narrative may be followed more easily.

Quotations are taken from the New Revised Standard Version.

1 The departure from Sinai

Numbers 10:11–36

The Israelites had spent nearly a year in the wilderness of Sinai (compare Exodus 19:1) and were now ready for the next phase of their journey to begin. The signal for them to depart was indicated by the lifting of the cloud 'from over the tabernacle of the covenant' (v. 11). After the cloud had lifted, the people set out by stages on a journey that would bring them, in the end, to the brink of the promised land itself. It was important for the Israelites that the tabernacle was to accompany them during the wilderness journey. Although there are some traditions in the Bible which indicate that God's presence could not be confined to a single place, the people of Israel believed that he was present in a special way in the tabernacle, just as he was later conceived as being present in a special way in the temple in Jerusalem. Significantly, the whole account of the revelation at Sinai in Exodus concludes with a report of God's glory entering the tabernacle (Exodus 40:34–38).

Moses asks Hobab, his father-in-law, to accompany the Israelites to the land of Canaan, presumably in order to act as a guide on the journey (v. 29). Hobab refuses at first, saying that he would prefer to return home to his family (v. 30). We are not told here what his final response was, but Judges 1:16 implies that he did eventually accede to Moses' request.

There are variant traditions in the Bible concerning the name of Moses' father-in-law. He is here called Hobab, but in Exodus 3:1 he is referred to as Jethro, and, to confuse matters even further, in Exodus 2:18 his name appears as Reuel. Various suggestions have been made to explain this apparent contradiction, but the discrepancy probably arises from the fact that there were independent traditions concerning Moses' father-in-law and that there was some uncertainty regarding his name.

The ark of the covenant—the visible manifestation of God's presence —preceded the Israelites on the journey (v. 33), and a cloud formed a protective covering for them by day, guarding them from the heat of the sun (v. 34). God was conceived as being enthroned upon the ark, and the call for him to 'arise' may reflect the battle cry used by the Israelites when they were engaged in war.

Moses' faith in this section stands in sharp contrast to the lack of faith exhibited by the people in the following chapters. Whereas he was sure God would do 'good' to Israel (v. 29), the people were convinced that he intended to do them harm (cf. 14:3).

2 Rebellion

Numbers 11:1–10, 18–23, 31–35

One of the recurring themes in the book of Numbers is the rebellion of the people against God and against their leader, Moses. In the first example of such rebellion (vv. 1–3), the cause of their complaint is not specified, although we may assume that it was the usual hardships of the desert march that precipitated their outburst. Whatever the precise cause of their rebellion, it clearly incurs God's displeasure, and his response is swift and decisive.

The fact that the next instance of rebellion follows immediately after the incident recorded in verses 1–3 suggests that the people had not learnt their lesson. In verses 4–10 they rebel again, and here the cause is made clear: the people are unhappy with the monotonous diet of manna that they are being given in the wilderness. In this instance, the discontent appears to have originated not with the Israelites themselves so much as with the 'rabble' that was among them. This probably refers to people of various nationalities who had accompanied the Israelites during the exodus and who had subsequently attached themselves to the Israelite camp. There is an alliteration in the Hebrew word for 'rabble', which might be most effectively reproduced in English by a term such as 'riff-raff'. Whoever instigated the rebellion on this occasion, however, they evidently wanted more nourishing sustenance than that which the desert could provide, and they begin to crave for the varied diet that they had enjoyed in Egypt (vv. 4b–6).

As so often when people look to the past, the Israelites remember only the good things. Time has already dulled their bitter memories of slavery, for they have clearly forgotten about the terrible conditions in which they were forced to live in Egypt, conditions described so graphically in

Exodus 1:11–14. In verses 18–23, the Israelites are promised a plentiful supply of meat, but it is suggested (rather ominously) that this will be something of a mixed blessing, for it will be given in such abundance that it will make them feel nauseated. As soon as the people start eating the quails that God provides, they are smitten with a plague (v. 33). This was deemed condign punishment for the people's inordinate craving, and, in memory of the event, the place where it occurred was called Kibroth-hattaavah, which means 'graves of craving'.

These stories provide a foretaste of what was to come, for the subsequent journey through the wilderness was frequently characterized by the people's obduracy and rebellion. The narratives provide a salutary reminder that whenever people show contempt and ingratitude towards the blessings that God has bestowed upon them, they must inevitably face the consequences.

3 Moses' helpers

Numbers 11:11–17, 24–30

Moses is clearly exasperated by the continual moaning of the people, and he feels that it is now his turn to complain. So he turns to God and, in his despair, vents his anger and frustration before him. He levels against God a series of reproaches cast in the form of rhetorical questions. Why has God dealt with his servant in such a malevolent manner? Why has he placed upon him such an intolerable burden (v. 11)? From where is Moses expected to obtain meat in the wilderness in order to satisfy the people's hunger (v. 13)? Moses' fierce outburst concludes with a simple confession: 'I am not able to carry all this people alone, for they are too heavy for me' (v. 14). Indeed, life has become so intolerable for him that he even pleads for God to kill him and have done with it (v. 15).

The story shows that when life appears too burdensome, God is always at hand to provide help and support. In this case, he instructs Moses to appoint 70 elders who 'shall bear the burden of the people along with you so that you will not bear it all by yourself' (v. 17). Moses brings the 70 elders to the tent of meeting (v. 24), where God takes some of the spirit resting on Moses and confers it on the elders who have been assembled. Equipped by the spirit, they begin to prophesy (v. 25). For some reason, two of the elders remain in the camp when the spirit is conferred upon the others; yet they too are able to prophesy, much to the irritation of Joshua, Moses' servant. When Joshua urges Moses to prevent them, the latter merely expresses the wish that all God's people would be prophets, endowed with the divine spirit (v. 29).

Clearly, according to this narrative, the phenomenon of prophecy was not to be confined rigidly to a favoured, chosen few; rather, it was a gift of God's spirit and, as such, should recognize no boundaries or limitations. The ideal expressed here is that all God's people should encounter the power of his energizing spirit, a wish that also finds expression in the great prophecy uttered by Joel: 'Then afterwards I will pour out my spirit on all flesh; your sons and your daughters shall prophesy, your old men shall dream dreams, and your young men shall see visions. Even on the male and female slaves, in those days, I will pour out my spirit' (Joel 2:28–29).

4 Moses' special position

Numbers 12:1–16

This chapter depicts the opposition of Miriam and Aaron to Moses on account of his marriage to a Cushite woman (v. 1) and because of his claim to possess a unique relationship with God (v. 2). A divine oracle vindicates Moses' position (vv. 6–8) and Miriam is struck down with leprosy for daring to oppose him (v. 10).

This story has often irritated feminist readers of the Bible, and it is easy to understand why. After all, both Aaron and Miriam were equally involved in casting doubts on Moses' exceptional position as God's intermediary, yet it is Miriam alone who is punished. In fact, the matter is not quite so straightforward. The verb 'spoke' in verse 1 is in the third person feminine singular in the Hebrew, which suggests that in the original version of the story it was Miriam alone who instigated the complaint regarding Moses' marriage, and the reference to Aaron was perhaps only added later by an editor.

Be that as it may, the story in its present form represents yet another rebellion—this time against Moses' supreme authority. It may seem, at first sight, a case of sibling rivalry and petty family jealousy, but in fact the rebellion had a much deeper significance. We must remember that the Bible depicts Miriam not only as Moses' sister but as a prophet in her own right (compare Exodus 15:20–21), and that it depicts Aaron not only as Moses' brother but also as the high priest and supreme religious leader of the people. Here, therefore, there is an alliance of priest and prophet challenging Moses' position as sole mediator between God and Israel. Moses himself does not respond to the complaint levelled by Miriam and Aaron, and it is left to God to silence the rebels. God tells them that he normally makes known his will to people through dreams and visions—that is, in enigmatic ways that need interpretation; however, this is 'not so with my servant Moses' (v. 7), for God has revealed his will to him in a much more direct and explicit fashion, 'face to face' and 'not in riddles'. Moses enjoyed a unique and intimate relationship with God and was even permitted to behold 'the form of the Lord' (v. 8).

There is a certain irony in the fact that Miriam and Aaron were forced to seek the mediation of the very one whose intimacy with God they had mistakenly called into question (vv. 11–12). Miriam was eventually cured of her leprosy, but only after being shut out of the camp for seven days (v. 15). In many ways, she stands out as one of the great heroines of the Old Testament, for she was one of the few women who, in a predominantly male-dominated society, felt confident enough to bid for the supreme position of community leadership, and felt no qualms about challenging male hegemony.

5 The story of the spies

Numbers 13:1–33

In this chapter, spies are sent out to gather intelligence about the land of Canaan prior to a military assault. Their names are given at length in verses 4–15. The spies are instructed to ascertain the military strength of the land ('whether the people who live in it are strong or weak', v. 18), the number of its inhabitants ('whether they are few or many', v. 18), its economic resources ('whether the land is rich or poor', v. 20) and its fertility ('whether there are trees in it or not', v. 20). The spies traverse the whole land of Canaan 'from the wilderness of Zin' in the far south to

Rehob in the far north (v. 21). It is impossible to calculate how far the spies travelled during their sojourn in Canaan. Although they evidently remained in the land for 40 days (v. 25), the figure 'forty' in the Bible is just a round number (similar to the number of years the Israelites spent in the wilderness) and is not to be taken too literally.

The report that the spies bring back begins on a positive note by drawing attention to the fertility of the land, which 'flows with milk and honey' (v. 27), but it soon emerges that the spies harbour serious reservations about entering the land to conquer it. Indeed, there is every indication that they sought to conduct a whispering campaign in order to undermine the hopes and aspirations of Moses and Aaron.

They observe that the towns are 'fortified and very large' and the people who inhabit them are 'strong' (v. 28). In order to drive home the point, they claim that they appeared very small and helpless by comparison: 'to ourselves we seemed like grasshoppers, and so we seemed to them' (v. 33). Caleb, one of the spies sent to reconnoitre the land (v. 6), does his best to put a positive gloss on the report and encourages the people to occupy the land, 'for we are well able to overcome it' (v. 30). However, his confidence in the people's ability to conquer the land is immediately rebuffed by the other spies, who are of the view that the inhabitants of Canaan will probably prove to be invincible (v. 31).

The prospect of invading such a land, especially for people who had already spent much time wandering through the desert, must have appeared bleak indeed. But it was bleak only because the words of encouragement that they had been given had fallen on deaf ears. The problem was that the people were more inclined to listen to words designed to instil in them a sense of disillusion and despair.

6 Rejecting God's plan of salvation

Numbers 14:1–10

Disconcerted by the negative report of the spies, the people begin to complain against Moses and Aaron and claim that they would rather have died in Egypt or in the wilderness than face the prospect of perishing by the sword in an attempt to conquer Canaan. They express a wish to return to captivity, if only to protect their wives and children from the atrocities of war (vv. 1–4).

So, just when the people are on the verge of entering the promised land, they resolve to appoint a new 'captain' who will lead them back to Egypt. Joshua and Caleb try to dissuade them by reminding them that Canaan is 'an exceedingly good land' (v. 7), and that there is no need to fear its inhabitants, for they can be annihilated as easily as bread can be devoured (v. 9). The difference between Israel and her adversaries is that God is present with his people, whereas the Canaanites will be denied the support and protection afforded by their gods. It all amounts to trust and confidence in God, and whether or not they are to believe the confession, 'the Lord is with us' (v. 9). But the encouraging words of Joshua and Caleb merely serve to aggravate the opposition against them, for the people decide to stone them to death, and the danger is averted only by the appearance of the 'glory of the Lord' at the tent of meeting (v. 10).

The depth of Israel's disillusionment is more apparent here than in any of the previous narratives, and it is important to realize precisely what was at stake. The Israelites had decided not only to replace their divinely appointed leader but also to reject God's entire plan of salvation for his people. No wonder Moses and Aaron fell to the ground in recognition of the affront that such disloyalty to God would entail (v. 5), and no wonder Joshua and Caleb 'tore their clothes' as a gesture of sorrow and distress for the attitude of the rebellious people (v. 6). The price of progress is often suffering and sacrifice, but this was clearly a price that the people of Israel were not prepared to pay.

Guidelines

A constant refrain of the people in our readings this week has been, 'Things were better in Egypt!' They remembered the fish, cucumbers, melons, leeks and onions that they ate 'for nothing' in Egypt (11:5), but had clearly forgotten all about the hardships they had to endure during their period of enslavement. Their selective memories made them view the past through rose-tinted spectacles, and all they could do was to hark back wistfully to 'the good old days'. The people had neither the courage nor the trust in God to face the future, and so they took refuge in the past. There is always a danger that in focusing too much on the past, we are hindered from moving confidently into the future. As I write these words, people throughout Wales have been celebrating the centenary of the great religious revival that swept the land in 1904; there has inevitably been a focus on our religious past, but there has been very little discussion on the direction in which the churches might move in the future.

The people of Israel could not understand why Moses had brought them out of Egypt into the wilderness to die in such misery. Every time anything went wrong, they began to grumble against God—Moses and Aaron often serving as scapegoats. True faith often involves a questioning of our own deeply held beliefs and an honest wrestling with what we perceive to be God's will for us. Yet, such struggling should never be allowed to deteriorate into an outright rebellion against his rule. There must come a time when, like Job, we submit to God's will, for if we do not, we court the risk of entering the arena of rebellion and deserting the arena of faith.

1 God's mercy and compassion

Numbers 14:11–25

Here God announces to Moses his intention to destroy the faithless Israelites and to create from Moses' descendants a greater and mightier nation. Moses, however, seeks to deter God from carrying out his intended judgment by appealing, firstly, to God's own standing and reputation among the nations (vv. 13–16) and, secondly, to his character as a merciful, forgiving and compassionate God (vv. 17–19). As a result of Moses' intercession, God relents and forgives the people (v. 20). At the same time, however, he vows that they will not go unpunished, for the rebels will die in the wilderness and none save Caleb will enter the promised land (vv. 23–24).

Clearly, the people lacked the trust and confidence that God was able to fulfil his promises, despite all the miracles that he had wrought on their behalf in Egypt and in the wilderness. The wonders of the exodus journey—the crossing of the Red Sea and the appearance of the manna—

15

should have led to an unconditional trust in God; instead, the people had shown their utter contempt for him by putting him to the test 'these ten times' (v. 22). We do not have ten stories of rebellion in Numbers, and it is probable that 'ten times' here just means 'often'.

What emerges in this narrative is God's unchanging love for his erring people, and nowhere is this clearer than in the first half of verse 18 ('The Lord is slow to anger, and abounding in steadfast love, forgiving iniquity and transgression'). Yet, the second half of the verse serves as a salutary reminder that God is able to punish as well as to pardon ('but by no means clearing the guilty, visiting the iniquity of the parents upon the children to the third and the fourth generation'). We see here Israel's belief that the strength of family ties was such that God's punishment could be transferred from one generation to another. Of course, the idea of making children pay for their parents' sin seems offensive to us, but it is worth remembering that other passages in the Old Testament affirm that each individual will bear the guilt for his or her own sin (compare Ezekiel 18).

Today's reading is of particular interest in that it reveals an important aspect of God's character: he is merciful, gracious, slow to anger, forgiving and abounding in steadfast love and faithfulness. This is a view of God's nature that is often (quite mistakenly) said to be found not in the Old Testament, but only in the New. The passage also indicates that God is able to change his mind and relent, which is important to remember, given that other biblical passages appear to advocate the unchangeableness of God's purpose.

2 God's punishment

Numbers 14:26–45

In verses 26–38, God vows that, as a punishment for their rebellion, all the people over 20 years old (except Caleb and Joshua) will die in the wilderness because of their lack of faith. Only their children will be permitted to enter the land of Canaan; in the meantime, the people are condemned to wander in the wilderness for 40 years—one year for every day that the spies had been in the land (v. 34). 'Forty years' is often used as a round number in the Old Testament to indicate a human lifetime;

here, it is thought of as the time needed for one generation of Israelites to die off. The spies who brought a negative report of the land, and who were ultimately responsible for the people's apostasy, are struck by a plague and die before the Lord (vv. 36–37). The passage is not without its bitter irony: those who had previously expressed a wish to die in the wilderness (14:2) will indeed be granted their request (vv. 28–30); conversely, the children who had been expected to perish in Canaan (v. 3) will be given possession of the promised land (v. 31).

In the brief narrative that follows (vv. 39–45), the people, having heard the divine sentence imposed upon them by God, express their remorse and resolve to win God's favour by attempting to enter the land of Canaan from the south. In doing so, however, they disregard Moses' warning that God will not help them; and the fact that the ark of the covenant—the traditional symbol of God's presence—remains in the camp is an ominous portent that the enterprise is doomed to failure (v. 44). In the event, the Israelites suffer a crushing defeat at the hands of the Amalekites and the Canaanites.

It is clear that the venture of the Israelites was doomed to fail not because of the strength of their enemies but because of an inherent weakness in themselves: they lacked trust in God and found themselves constantly rebelling against his will and disobeying his commands. They had turned their backs on God, so he would now turn his back on them. The message of the passage is clear: people who lack God's favour and blessing cannot hope to prosper.

3 The offering of sacrifice

Numbers 15:1–21

Chapter 15 contains a miscellaneous collection of laws that appear to bear no obvious connection either with the story of the spies in chapters 13—14 or with the narrative concerning the rebellion of Korah, Dathan and Abiram which follows in chapters 16—17. Yet, the laws contained here may be regarded as a pertinent comment upon the incidents related in the previous chapters: despite the manifest unbelief of the people and their presumptuous attempt to take the land (14:39–45), God's promises had not been completely annulled. If only the people were

17

prepared to indicate their repentance by offering the appropriate sacrifices, they would indeed be brought into the land of Canaan (vv. 2, 18) and would experience once again God's abundant blessings.

Verses 1–16 lay down the quantities of flour, oil and wine that were to accompany the different forms of public and private sacrifices. The amounts evidently related to the size of the animal: the more valuable the animal sacrificed, the more costly the gift that was to accompany it. The custom of offering such accompaniments to a sacrifice is well attested in the Old Testament. We recall that Hannah took to Shiloh 'a three-year-old bull, an ephah of flour, and a skin of wine' (1 Samuel 1:24). The aim of the sacrifice was to make a 'pleasing odour for the Lord' (v. 3), and this reflects the primitive idea that the deity actually smells and takes delight in the sacrifice. The Israelites were taught to give a place in their worship to pleasing odours, and the use of incense by some parts of the Christian church today is a reflection of this custom.

In verses 17–21, Moses instructs the people to make a 'donation to the Lord' whenever they eat 'of the bread of the land' (v. 19). At each new baking, the people were to present a loaf as an offering to God. Significantly, the principle of giving offerings is here brought directly into the domestic life of the Israelites.

It is perhaps worth noting that the regulations in verses 1–21 were to apply only 'when you come into the land you are to inhabit' (v. 2; compare v. 18), and the 'flour, wine and oil' which were to accompany the sacrifices presuppose a settled life in Canaan, where such products were readily available. Thus, whereas the people had been constantly looking back nostalgically to their life in Egypt, these laws look forward hopefully to their settlement in the promised land. The laws may thus be understood as an affirmation that God would eventually bring his people into Canaan, and that he would indeed fulfil the promise he had made to Abraham that his descendants would inherit the land.

4 Inadvertent offences

Numbers 15:22–31

These verses deal with the offerings to be made in the case of inadvertent transgressions. If such offences had been perpetrated by the community as a whole (vv. 22–26), a young bull was to be presented as a burnt offering (together with the appropriate amount of grain offerings and drink offerings), and a male goat was to be presented as a sin offering. If the offences had been perpetrated by an individual (vv. 27–29), the only requirement was that a female goat be presented as a sin offering. The passage contains no specific example of the type of offence envisaged, nor does it indicate how the transgression might have been brought to light; its concern is only with the measures to be taken to remove the guilt that had been incurred.

The passage is of interest in that it distinguishes between sins committed inadvertently or unconsciously and those committed deliberately and intentionally. The former were to be dealt with in a sympathetic and understanding way because the act was perpetrated 'in error' (v. 29). However, the sacrificial system provided no means of expiation for those who had committed an offence in deliberate defiance of God's will. The latter were considered to have behaved in such an abominable manner that the only recourse was to excommunicate them from the community (v. 31). They had 'despised the word of the Lord' and had effectively cut themselves off from any meaningful relationship with God and with his people.

Today's reading serves as a reminder of the need to exhibit a certain generosity of spirit in our dealings with unwitting offenders. It also serves to remind us of the seriousness of deliberately flouting God's will. The dire warning contained in this passage is echoed in the letter to the Hebrews: 'For if we wilfully persist in sin after having received the knowledge of the truth, there no longer remains a sacrifice for sins' (Hebrews 10:26).

5 Breaking the sabbath ✓

13/01

Numbers 15:32–36

This short narrative may have been inserted at this point because it provided a concrete example of a person who had committed a sin wilfully and deliberately. The sin in question involved gathering wood on the sabbath. The man found guilty of the offence was brought before Moses, Aaron and the whole congregation for trial, but because Moses did not know how to deal with the case, the accused had to be placed in custody while guidance was sought from God. The penalty pronounced by divine decree was death by stoning, and the passage ends by noting that the sentence was duly carried out.

The fact that the case involving the wood-gatherer had to be adjourned 'because it was not clear what should be done to him' (v. 34) seems strange, for Exodus 31:14–15 and 35:2–3 had already prescribed the death penalty for failure to observe the sabbath. The point here may be that the people sought clarification as to the mode of execution required by the law. Be that as it may, the keeping of the sabbath was regarded as so important that its breach meant that one's very life was at stake.

It is interesting to observe that the whole community was involved in ensuring that the transgressor was duly punished, and in this way everyone shared equal responsibility for his death. Our own system of 'trial by jury' is similarly intended to ensure that a representative sample of the community is involved in deciding the guilt or innocence of a particular offender.

The passage provides an important lesson on the subject of sabbath observance. Here, the breaking of the sabbath is regarded as an offence comparable to blasphemy (compare Leviticus 24:10–23) or idolatry (Deuteronomy 17:2–7), which similarly required the death penalty to be imposed. Of course, we may well think that the Hebrews had gone to extreme measures to ensure observance of the sabbath, but we would do well to ponder whether we have not gone to the other extreme in allowing Sunday to be treated just like any other day. Jesus respected the ancient commandment to 'remember the sabbath day, and keep it holy' (Exodus 20:8), yet he insisted that the sabbath was not intended to be an intolerable burden, but was God's merciful provision for humankind (Mark 2:27).

6 The wearing of tassels

Numbers 15:37–41

In this passage, Moses is instructed to command the people to 'make fringes on the corners of their garments... and to put a blue cord on the fringe at each corner' (v. 38). Whether the Hebrew text refers to a continuous fringe, as the translation of the NRSV suggests, or whether the piece of clothing in question was one with four tassels attached to each corner (as suggested by the translation of the REB and NIV) is unclear, but the fringe or tassels were intended to serve as a continual reminder of the need to obey God's will.

The wearing of tassels at the corners of garments was an ancient custom practised by other nations in antiquity. Egyptian and Meso-potamian sculptures have been discovered, dating from the first and second millennia BC, which depict garments with tassels hanging from them, although it is not clear whether these tassels were merely decorative or whether they served a specific purpose (such as warding off evil spirits). Their significance in Israel, however, was quite clear: they served as a visible reminder of the need for continued allegiance to God and obedience to his commands. They also functioned as a warning not to follow 'the lust of your own heart and your own eyes' (v. 39). Deuteronomy 6:6–9 commands that the Israelites should bind the commandments on their hands and their foreheads, signifying the need to remember God at all times. The wearing of tassels remained important in New Testament times (compare Matthew 23:5) and the custom still survives today among orthodox Jews who continue to wear a 'tallith'—an oblong piece of cloth with a hole in the middle for passing over the head and a tassel attached to each corner.

The object of wearing the tassels was that every time the people looked at them, they would 'remember all the commandments of the Lord and do them' (v. 39). We sometimes tie a piece of string on a finger—often in order to remember some very trivial things. What we need are aids to remind us of the need to remain constantly in a right relationship with God.

Guidelines

The readings this week continue the theme of rebellion and underline the seriousness of disobeying God's will. In fact, some of the passages studied have illustrated the classic biblical theme of faithlessness and its punishment. As far as the people of Israel were concerned, their punishment entailed a delay of 40 years before they (or, rather, their children) could enter the land of Canaan. Because of their lack of trust in God's guidance, the people themselves were responsible for their exclusion from the promised land. By expressing a desire to return to Egypt, they had rejected everything that God had done for them in liberating them from slavery and providing for their needs. No wonder God's patience was wearing thin: 'How long will this people despise me? And how long will they refuse to believe in me, in spite of all the signs that I have done among them?' (14:11). Usually in the Old Testament, questions beginning with the words 'How long?' are addressed by humans to God (for example, Psalm 13:1–2); here, however, such questions are addressed by God to the people in sheer exasperation. Would they never learn from their experiences? Would it never dawn on them that God's dealings with his people were intended to inspire faith, trust and obedience? Instead of pondering over their actions, learning from their mistakes and changing their attitude, the people had become even more stubborn and self-righteous.

Yet, despite this obduracy, we have seen in our readings a message of hope that God's ultimate purpose will not be thwarted, however hard people try to frustrate his designs. And this hope is ultimately based on the character of God himself, a God who is 'slow to anger, and abounding in steadfast love, forgiving iniquity and transgression' (14:18).

1 Korah's rebellion

Numbers 16:1–11, 16–24, 31–35

Numbers 16 is a long and, in many ways, perplexing chapter, and it seems best to limit our readings to a few sections rather than trying to take the chapter as a whole. The confusion arises from the fact that, in all probability, two different stories of rebellion have been interwoven here, and as a result the chapter inevitably betrays a certain lack of cohesion. The first story, which appears in verses 1–11, 16–24 and (parts of) 31–35, records a rebellion against the religious authority of Moses and Aaron by a certain Korah (of the tribe of Levi) and 250 leaders of the congregation. The second story is contained, for the most part, in verses

12–15, 25–30 and (parts of) 31–35, and relates a purely secular rebellion by Dathan and Abiram against Moses' leadership. A later editor has rather clumsily tried to combine the two accounts at various points (for example, by mentioning all three protagonists together in verses 1 and 24), and this has inevitably resulted in much confusion.

The rebellion by Korah and his followers was evidently motivated by jealousy and resentment. Korah and his followers were Levites, but they were not content with having to occupy what they regarded as an inferior position and were intent upon trying to secure for themselves the rights and privileges that pertained to the priesthood. Moses responds by challenging them to undertake a specifically priestly task: the offering of incense. By the way in which God received the incense offering, it would be made known who was holy and entitled to draw near to him (vv. 5–7). In verses 8–11, Moses emphasizes that, by being entrusted with the levitical service in the tabernacle, Korah and his companions have already been give preferential treatment over the rest of the congregation, and with this they ought to be satisfied. In vaunting their claim to a share in the priestly office, it is not the authority of Aaron that they are challenging but the authority of God himself.

Verse 22 is particularly interesting for two reasons. In the first place, God is here described as the 'God of the spirits of all flesh': that is, he is regarded not only as the God of Israel but as the God of 'all mankind', as the REB puts it. This is important, for the view (often advanced) that the Jewish community was introverted and advocated a stringent separatism from all other peoples represents only half the truth; there is also the belief that the nations of the world would ultimately turn to God and that his kingship would extend over all peoples (compare Psalms 47; 93; 96). Secondly, the question addressed to God ('shall one person sin and you become angry with the whole congregation?') appears to advocate the notion of individual responsibility for one's sin. There is perhaps a deliberate rejection here of an earlier idea that was once current in Israel—that many could suffer for the guilt of one person. That notion was later felt to be unjust, and it was left to prophets such as Ezekiel to emphasize that each individual was responsible for his or her own sins (compare Ezekiel 18).

2 The rebellion of Dathan and Abiram

Numbers 16:12–15, 25–35

As noted above, these verses appear to recount a different rebellion, for here it is Dathan and Abiram (rather than Korah) who rebel, and the rebellion this time appears to be against Moses' leadership. When Moses summons them to appear before him, they contemptuously ignore his demand, accusing him of misleading the people and arrogantly assuming for himself the role of leader. They even accuse him of having brought the people to the wilderness 'out of a land flowing with milk and honey' in order to kill them (v. 13). The phrase 'land flowing with milk and honey' occurs often in the Old Testament, but it usually refers to the land of Canaan; here, however, it is used to refer to Egypt. The rebels evidently regarded the fertile land whence they came, rather than the unknown country to which they were being led, as the 'promised land'. They accuse Moses of being a deceiver, beguiling them with false promises. Their words serve to express not only their doubts concerning the whole enterprise of the exodus, but also their utter contempt for God's plan of salvation for his people.

The story continues in verses 25–35. Moses, accompanied by the elders of Israel, goes into the tents of Dathan and Abiram, and announces a test that will decide the question of his authority once and for all. If nothing unusual happens, and the rebels die a natural death, then it will have been shown that they were correct, and that Moses' leadership is, indeed, self-assumed. But if, on the other hand, God intervenes in a miraculous way and destroys the rebels, then it will be proved that Moses' authority is by divine appointment. Verses 31 and 33 indicate that no sooner had Moses finished speaking than the ground swallowed up all the rebels and they descended into Sheol, the realm of the dead.

What unites the two stories contained in chapter 16 is that both represent a struggle for power and influence. The story of Korah represents a struggle for religious power, and no doubt such struggles were common during the later period of Israel's history. The story of Dathan and Abiram represents a secular rebellion of the type encountered all too frequently in the central portion of Numbers: they resented the fact that Moses appeared to be lording it over the people. The two stories serve as a reminder that power struggles occur in all communities, both religious and secular, but they also serve to teach us the importance of coming to a proper understanding of our own importance and the danger of arrogating to ourselves positions above our station.

3 Aaron's rod

18/a ✓

Numbers 17:1–13

The challenge to Korah and his company to present incense before God (16:6–7, 17), and the dire consequences that followed (16:31–35), should have proved beyond doubt that their overweening ambition was misplaced. But the congregation reacted merely by accusing Moses and Aaron of having 'killed the people of the Lord' (16:41). God therefore has to provide a further demonstration of the privileged status of the Levites.

Moses is instructed to take a rod from each of the tribal leaders, and to inscribe on each rod the name of the tribe to which it belonged (vv. 1–3). He is then to place the rods in the tent of meeting in front of the ark of the covenant (v. 4) and is told that the rod of the person whom God has chosen will sprout (v. 5). Moses does as he is commanded (vv. 6–7) and on the following day he finds that the rod of Aaron, representing the tribe of Levi, has not only sprouted, but has blossomed and produced ripe almonds (v. 8). God then commands that Aaron's rod should be placed in the sanctuary as a permanent reminder of the elevated status of the Levites, and as a warning to those who, in future, might be tempted to rebel (v. 10).

The rod in the Old Testament was a symbol of power and authority (cf. Exodus 4:1–5). The miracle recorded in this chapter, then, was God's way of saying that his authority, as far as the priesthood was concerned, was vested in Aaron and in him alone. Significantly, the chapter concludes with the people crying out for mercy: 'We are perishing; we are lost, all of us are lost!' (v. 12). At long last they appear to have understood that they need someone to draw near to God on their behalf and to make atonement for their sins. In other words, they recognize the need for the priesthood, and the next chapter shows that they were ready to pay for it by offering the necessary tithes and first fruits.

4 The duties and rewards of the clergy

Numbers 18:1–32

Instructions concerning the duties of the priests and Levites are presented in the form of an address by God to Aaron (vv. 1–7). That Aaron should be addressed directly by God is unusual, for elsewhere God's instructions to him are regularly mediated through Moses (compare 6:22–23; 8:1–2).

The remainder of the chapter (vv. 8–32) is primarily concerned to establish the means of support for the clergy, and, to this end, a list is given of the gifts that the priests (vv. 8–20, 25–32) and the Levites (vv. 21–24) were entitled to receive in return for the services rendered at the sanctuary. The priests were to receive those parts of the grain, sin and guilt offerings which were not burnt on the altar (v. 9), together with all the elevation offerings (v. 11) and all the best of the oil, wine and grain (v. 12). They were also to be given the new produce of the year that was dedicated to God (vv. 13–14). The Hebrew term here translated 'devoted thing' was a technical term designating something that was to be entirely withdrawn from ordinary secular use and given over to the deity; the thing was henceforth regarded as his exclusive possession and could not, therefore, be redeemed or disposed of in any way. Here, the term refers to the voluntary offerings which the people had dedicated to God, and which could not thereafter be redeemed.

Moreover, the priests were entitled to appropriate the redemption money paid for the human firstborn and the firstborn of unclean animals (v. 15). The firstlings of clean animals could not be redeemed by the payment of money, so they had to be sacrificed, but their flesh then became the property of the priests (vv. 17–18). Any member of the priest's family could eat some of the offerings, provided that they were ceremonially clean (vv. 11–13, 19). Of course, all the offerings mentioned were, in the first instance, the property of God, but he gave them to the priests as compensation for the fact that they could possess no landed property in Canaan (v. 20). By means of the offerings that were presented to them, a 'covenant of salt' was established between God and the priests (v. 19). It is generally agreed that this phrase denotes a covenant which was regarded as eternal and indissoluble. The origin of this unusual expression is unclear but some suggest that it derives from the common use of salt as a preservative in the ancient world, the commodity thus becoming a symbol of permanence and durability.

The Levites, who were similarly to be deprived of territorial inheritance, were to receive all the tithes presented by the people (vv. 21–24); however, they were obliged to give a tenth part of this ('a tithe of the tithe') to the priests (v. 26), thus furnishing the latter with an additional source of revenue. The tithe (that is, the exaction of a tenth of one's produce) was a phenomenon widely attested in the ancient Near East; in Israel, the custom may have originated as a royal tax before it came to be regarded as a sacral due payable to the temple and its personnel.

This chapter establishes the principle that priests must be allowed to derive their income from the service they render to God. Significantly, Paul indicates his approval of this system of financial support (1 Corinthians 9:13–14). The lesson for the apostle's readers should be clear: 'those who proclaim the gospel should get their living by the gospel'.

5 The red heifer

Numbers 19:1–22

The Israelites are here commanded to bring an unblemished red heifer to Eleazar the priest, and the animal is to be slaughtered in his presence outside the camp (vv. 1–3). After sprinkling some of its blood seven times towards the front of the tent of meeting (v. 4), the animal is completely burned (v. 5), and from its ashes a mixture is prepared which is used for cleansing a person from any defilement occasioned by contact with the dead (vv. 11–13).

Verses 14–22 contain further detailed instructions concerning the use of the mixture in a variety of specific instances. Defilement could be caused without necessarily coming into direct, physical contact with the dead (v. 14). Moreover, the defilement caused by the dead was considered to be so contagious that it was capable of affecting material objects as well as living beings (v. 15).

The belief that contact with the dead rendered a person ritually unclean was both ancient and widespread, and the possibility of being purified from such contamination is alluded to in several passages in the

Old Testament (compare 6:6–12). However, only here in the Old Testament is the ritual of the red heifer described, although the rite is evidently presupposed in 31:21–24. The ritual has no exact parallel in antiquity, but there is some evidence to suggest that the Romans used the ashes of a slaughtered calf in ceremonies of purification. It is thought that the ritual described in this chapter was magical in origin, but that it was later imbued with a religious significance: uncleanness occasioned by contact with the dead was an affront to God's holiness, and had to be removed by means of ritual purification. It seems that, as far as the people of Israel were concerned, cleanliness really was next to godliness.

In New Testament times, the belief persisted that contact with the dead rendered a person unclean. This is why, in Jesus' day, tombs were whitewashed or marked by chalk, lest the unwary should walk on them without realizing that they were being defiled (compare Matthew 23:27; Luke 11:44). The author of the letter to the Hebrews refers to the rite described in this passage in order to draw a contrast with the sacrifice of Jesus on the cross: 'For if the blood of goats and bulls, with the sprinkling of the ashes of a heifer, sanctifies those who have been defiled so that their flesh is purified, how much more will the blood of Christ, who through the eternal Spirit offered himself without blemish to God, purify our conscience from dead works to worship the living God!' (Hebrews 9:13–14).

6 Water from the rock

Numbers 20:1–13

Our final reading opens with a report of the death and burial of Miriam (v. 1) and proceeds to record one final incident of rebellion on the part of the people. This time they complain about the lack of water, and they reproach Moses for having brought them into the wilderness. The hardship endured by them was such that they wished they had suffered the same fate as their kindred who had 'died before the Lord' (v. 3), a clear reference to the destiny that befell some of the Israelites at the time of Korah's rebellion (cf. 16:35, 49).

Moses is instructed by God to take a rod and to command an adjacent rock to yield water. He takes the rod and strikes the rock twice, whereupon water gushes forth in such abundance that the congregation and the livestock are satiated (v. 11). In doing this, however, both Moses and Aaron are said to have offended against the Lord and, as a punishment, they are prevented from leading the people into the promised land (v. 12).

The nature of the transgression committed by Moses and Aaron, which prevented them from entering the promised land, is by no means clear in the text as it stands. One possibility is that Moses was guilty of disobedience. After all, he had been instructed by God merely to speak to the rock (v. 8), but instead he struck it with the rod (v. 11), an act that constituted disobedience to the divine command; indeed, his insubordination was augmented by the fact that he struck the rock twice, evidently believing that a single stroke was not enough! Another possibility is that Moses' sin lay in the rhetorical question uttered by him in verse 10: 'Listen, you rebels, shall we bring water for you out of this rock?' By implying that it was they—Moses and Aaron—who had the ability to provide water from the rock, he failed to give God the credit for the miracle that was about to happen, and sought to prevent the divine power from being manifested to the people. Neither explanation is completely satisfactory, but it is clear from verse 12 that the leaders of the people, like the rest of their generation, had been guilty of the sin of unbelief ('because you did not trust in me'), and that their punishment, likewise, was to die in the wilderness.

The incident recorded in this passage is highly significant, for it serves to explain why Moses and Aaron were denied the privilege of leading the people into the promised land. Clearly, disobedience was no less serious for Moses, the man of God, than it was for Israel, the people of God. It is worth recalling the psalmist's comment on the incident described in this passage: 'They angered the Lord at the waters of Meribah, and it went ill with Moses on their account; for they made his spirit bitter, and he spoke words that were rash' (Psalm 106:32–33).

22/01

Guidelines

The readings this week have covered a variety of different topics, and the reader may well be forgiven for wondering how relevant they are for the society in which we live. Yet these chapters frequently contain profound truths, provided we are willing to scratch a little below the surface. Take, for example, chapter 18, which lists in a rather tedious fashion the duties and dues of the priests and Levites. This chapter might appear to bear little relevance today but, in fact, it establishes an important principle: the need to provide proper and adequate support for those engaged in the service of God. Significantly, Jesus said that 'the labourer deserves to be paid' as he sent out the 70 disciples to preach the gospel (Luke 10:7), and in a similar vein Paul stated that 'those who proclaim the gospel should get their living by the gospel' (1 Corinthians 9:14).

Further, Numbers 18 also contains a reference to tithing, and it is worth remembering that the custom of contributing a tenth of one's income has persisted in some quarters of the Christian church to this day as an ideal by which Christians measure their giving. Perhaps the problem today is that many Christians are content to give merely a 'tithe of the tithe' (18:26) to support good causes. Unless and until the level of Christian giving raises dramatically, the church will always lack the material resources needed to tackle global poverty and to continue its redemptive ministry in the world.

FURTHER READING

Eryl W. Davies, *Numbers* (New Century Bible Commentary), Marshall Pickering, 1995.

B. Maarsingh, *Numbers: A Practical Commentary*, Eerdmans, 1987.

Walter Riggans, *Numbers*, The Saint Andrew Press, 1983.

Gordon J. Wenham, *Numbers* (Tyndale Old Testament Commentaries), Inter-Varsity Press, 1981.

WORSHIP

'Let God be God,' said the great Swiss theologian Karl Barth. If we follow that advice, we will find ourselves at the best possible starting point for an exploration of Christian worship. For, at its heart, worship is about nothing other than the creature's willing acknowledgment of the creator, the response of the finite to the infinite.

Unfortunately, as a term and a concept, 'worship' has tended to suffer for a long time from usage that is too specific. The journalist Ysenda Maxtone Graham describes her bemusement on her trip around different churches in the Church of England:

'We'll pray for a little bit longer, and then we'll look to the Lord in worship'. Leaders of evangelical services say this, and... soon you realize that 'look to the Lord in worship' means 'sing'. When someone in a jersey comes up to you after the service and says, 'Hi. I'm in charge of worship here,' he means, 'I'm in charge of the music'. Rather like 'gay', the word is past saving. It has taken on a new specialized meaning, and even those who regret this have given in.

This is a particularly pessimistic view, but it makes the point. For sure, music has a crucial role to play in any complete understanding of worship (as we will discover in our studies through the coming days), but the very word 'worship' needs to be redeemed from such limited associations.

Of course, it is possible to overreact to a definition that is too narrow, and opt instead for a view that ends up being too broad to be of any concrete meaning or use. Nevertheless, any truly biblical view of worship will inevitably involve the offering not only of our prayer, praise and penitence, but also of our whole selves in a life of faith (Romans 12), and of love for God and neighbour.

Over the coming days we will be exploring aspects of the church's corporate liturgical life. In doing so, however, we must not lose sight of this all-encompassing call, the call that comes at the end of each service of holy communion, to 'go in peace to love and serve the Lord'.

Quotations are taken from the New Revised Standard Version.

Worship and mission

1 Creation's purpose, momentum and goal

Psalm 148

Human decisions and actions affect not only other humans, but the world as a whole. The current ecological crises faced by our planet show us the power that we humans have to save or stifle the creation in which we live. But what does the Bible say? Jeremy Begbie, speaking of God's covenant love for creation, summarizes thus: 'Where do we fit into this grand cosmic drama? The Bible speaks many times of creation praising God: it is our role to extend that worship, to enable creation to glorify its Maker in a way that it could never do if it were left to itself.'

There are really two points at stake. First, the whole cosmos was made primarily to worship its maker (e.g. Psalm 96:12; 98:8–9; Isaiah 44:23). The poet Gerard Manley Hopkins saw this when he wrote that 'the world is charged with the grandeur of God', and the writer Evelyn Underhill began her classic study *Worship* with these words:

Worship, in all its grades and kinds, is the response of the creature to the Eternal. Nor need we limit this definition to the human sphere. There is a sense in which we may think of the whole life of the universe, seen and unseen, conscious and unconscious, as an act of worship, glorifying its Origin, Sustainer, and End.

The second point is equally important, however. Human beings are the mouthpiece, the megaphone, for the worship of creation. Part of our special God-given calling as human beings, made in 'the image of God', is to look after creation in such a way that its praise will be articulated and received by God. We are, in effect, the priests of creation.

This immediately challenges us at the day-to-day level: how we behave and what we choose in the aisles of our supermarkets turns out to be at least as important as how we sing and pray in the aisles and pews of our churches. We cannot sustain a view of the natural world that is merely utilitarian. We are Christians first and foremost, not consumers.

2 Mission as the servant of worship ✓

Humans are not only called to offer the world's worship to God, and to reflect his image back to him in thanks and praise. We are also called to offer God's grace and salvation to the world in mission. These are two sides of the same coin, the coin of what it means to be human. But is one side more important than the other?

Sometimes churches tend to sell the idea that mission is the most important thing in the world. Worship, especially corporate acts of worship centred on word and sacrament, is a means to a missionary end. But from the viewpoint of the Bible, this is back to front. For instance, Isaiah's vision of God's people as the 'light of the nations' has to be seen in the context of the ultimate vision, that of all nations streaming up to Jerusalem to worship God. Likewise, the letter to the Ephesians looks ahead to the time when all things will be gathered together under the rule of Christ (Ephesians 1:10). In other words, centrifugal mission is relative ⏋ to centripetal worship.

The 17th-century *Westminster Shorter Catechism* begins with the question 'What is the chief end of man?' to which the answer is given, 'Man's chief end is to glorify God, and to enjoy him for ever.' The modern American preacher John Piper has unpacked this same point:

All of history is moving toward one great goal, the white-hot worship of God and his Son among all the peoples of the earth. Missions exist because worship doesn't. Worship is ultimate, not mission, because God is ultimate, not man… When this age is over, and the countless millions of the redeemed fall on their faces before the throne of God, mission will be no more. It is a temporary necessity. But worship abides forever.

Do these priorities underlie our own view of the church and the world? Are the worship and fellowship of our own local Christian community things to which people are drawn? If not, why not? While both are vital, are we nevertheless better at simply meeting people where they are, or at helping to lead them *into* the life of God's kingdom?

3 Declaring the greatness of God ✓ 25/1

Psalm 135

For countless music lovers, the pinnacle of Handel's oratorio *Messiah* is the great 'Hallelujah Chorus'. The single word (in Hebrew meaning 'Praise the Lord') is repeated over and over again by the full chorus, with trumpet and drums adding the final touch to the jubilant mood. Yet the lyrics comprise more than this one single word. They go on to spell out just why it is that the Lord deserves such praise: 'For the Lord God omnipotent reigneth.' He is 'King of kings and Lord of lords' and he will 'reign for ever and ever'.

Our praise and worship of God ought always to be rooted in an acknowledgment of who God really is, and what he has done for us. God is the subject, and not only the object of worship. As Marva Dawn points out, 'Worship is about God inviting us into his presence, not the priest inviting us into his living room.' Or, to put it another way, God 'opens our lips' first, and only then can we 'proclaim his praise' (Psalm 51:15).

For this reason, the book of Psalms never gives us example of abstract praise (a mere 'Alleluia' for the sake of it); instead, the Psalms provide countless reasons why such praise is due. The great preacher John Stott talks about psalms such as the one we meet today (Psalm 135) as being 'Alleluia sandwiches'—with exhortations and shouts of praise at either end, and the meaty explanation in the middle.

Unlike a mere idol, God is powerful enough to do as he pleases. Not only is he innately good, but he is also all-powerful, controlling the natural world and acting decisively on behalf of his chosen people.

Look through the Psalter for other examples of 'Alleluia sandwiches', and then be alert to other examples in the Bible where praise is not simply spoken into thin air, but is connected, as if by an umbilical cord, to the very being and action of God (e.g. Exodus 15:1–21). If we speak or sing our praises merely into thin air, forgetting who the true God really is, then we are likely to end up worshipping other false gods, and reflecting their image instead. But if our diet of worship includes whole sandwiches, we will better avoid the traps of idolatry.

34

4 Filling out a theology of worship

Romans 12:1–13

In the parish of Bemerton near Salisbury, the 17th-century priest and poet George Herbert would encourage his flock to attend Morning and Evening Prayer each day, not just on Sunday. In one of his most famous hymns he pledges to praise God 'seven whole days, not one in seven'. And while, for most Christians, Sunday may be the day on which corporate prayer and worship find their focus, and the day that provides greatest nourishment from word and sacrament, it is well not to neglect the need for regular corporate prayer and fellowship throughout the week.

However, there is more to Romans 12 (and to a biblical view of daily worship) than this. Presenting ourselves as 'living sacrifices' involves the transformation of our whole outlook on the world, so that we might know what God would have us be and do in every area of life. We respond to what he has done with what one writer has called 'praise and thanksliving', and this extends not only to our love for other Christians ('contribute to the needs of the saints') but outward to include 'hospitality to strangers' (v. 13).

The Bible reserves some of its most scathing invective for the shallow spirituality that fails to connect the 'service' of liturgy with the 'service' of discipleship. The prophet Hosea reminds a pious but rebellious people that God desires 'steadfast love and not sacrifice, the knowledge of God rather than burnt-offerings' (Hosea 6:6). Micah makes a similar point (Micah 6:8), and in the early church the apostle James was keen to show how faith and works are really two sides of the same coin.

The chorister's prayer, therefore, serves equally well not only for those who lead our corporate worship but for any Christian seeking to connect worship and the world, on the threshold of another busy and demanding week:

> *Bless, O Lord, us Thy servants, who minister in Thy temple. Grant that what we sing with our lips, we may believe in our hearts, and what we believe in our hearts, we may show forth in our lives. Through Jesus Christ our Lord. Amen.*

5 Freedom and liturgy ✓ 29/(

1 Corinthians 14:23–33

The Holy Spirit is the Spirit of order and also the Spirit of freedom. The apostle Paul seems to see no intrinsic tension here. His description of corporate worship is marked by flexibility and variety, yet he feels he must challenge disorder because of his understanding of God (v. 33) and his concern for a credible link between worship and mission (vv. 23–25).

It often seems like an uphill struggle to relate order and freedom in the worshipping life of our churches. So-called 'liturgical' churches can be tempted to accuse so-called 'Spirit-led' congregations of chaos and lack of reverence. The counter-accusation is often that ordered liturgy can become predictable and stifling—a mere 'going through the motions'. But, of course, every church *becomes* liturgical over time, with certain patterns and habits, even if these are largely unconscious or unacknowledged. And from the earliest examples of written and crafted prayers and songs (Philippians 2:5–11; Colossians 1:15–20), through to new and creative liturgy being tried out for the first time in our own day, there is much to be said for the use of carefully thought-out and well written words and music. As one liturgist has put it, in the recorded words of the Church's heritage we have:

> … *the accumulated wisdom and beauty of the Christian Church, the garnered excellence of many saints. We are by them released from the accidents of time and place. Above all we are preserved against the worst dangers of selfishness; in the common prayer we join together in a great fellowship that is as wide as the world, and we are guided, not by the limited notions of our own minister, nor by the narrow impulses of our own desires, but by the mighty voice that rises from the general heart of Christendom.*

Percy Dearmer

Of course, the Spirit of freedom and order is also the Spirit of other similar balances—for example, the need to embrace both reverence and rejoicing. In 2 Samuel 6:1–11 we read that King David *fears* the holy God, but *rejoices* in the grace and love of God. The Hebrew word for 'rejoice' is the same as that for 'dance', and we all sometimes feel compelled to dance and sing with abandon and spontaneity, like David before the ark. Even looking like a fool can become a real mark of a life touched by God. The bishop of Durham, Tom Wright, has said, 'We all reach a point where somebody else's enthusiasm strikes us as over the top. But let's face it, the whole point of enthusiasm is that it's over the top.'

We are called to lay aside the self-regard and self-security that leave no room for the fragile and the funny. In taking ourselves seriously as God's children, we must paradoxically also learn to take ourselves less seriously, learning to wonder and rejoice in the God who loves us and blesses us.

28/1

6 Coming back to the (eucharistic) heart of worship

Mark 14:12–26

When Jesus met with his disciples on the night before his betrayal, we know that the meal they shared was already well-rooted in Hebraic liturgical tradition. Fellowship, food and worship all blended together in the Passover supper, and in Mark's account we even hear of them singing a hymn afterwards (v. 26).

Jesus took this meal and crammed it with extra levels of meaning. In the Lord's Supper we participate in the very life of God through Christ (1 Corinthians 10:16), and we show forth the saving death of Christ to the world (1 Corinthians 11:26) in what amounts to a 'visible word'. More than that, we appropriate the benefits of the *past* work of Christ; in the *present* our individual and corporate life is nourished by his life-giving Spirit; and we are even granted a foretaste of the *future* banquet of heaven. We receive God's blessings through this sign and means of grace, and we offer ourselves and our world in a living sacrifice of praise of thanksgiving (the word 'eucharist' means literally 'thanksgiving'). This latter point can appear controversial to many, and the Reformation sought to counter any suggestion that we offer a contribution towards our own salvation, or that the church can possibly add to the unique sacrifice of Christ. But consider the following points:

• The Lord's Supper involves bread and wine, not simply grain and grapes. In other words, we accept with empty hands the gifts of God in creation as a means of his grace, and yet we also offer back to him that which, through that same grace, human hands have shaped and transformed. 'All things come from you and of your own have we given you' (1 Chronicles 29:14).

- However we choose to understand Jesus' words 'this is my body/blood', we cannot fail to catch the connection Jesus is making between the bread and wine of the supper and his own self, offered the very next day for the redemption of the world.

The eucharist is the most priestly act, the most human act, the most intercessory act of all—the point at which God and the world are most clearly offered to one another through the prayerful action of the church. No wonder the church has never even tried to survive without it. As one writer has said:

Was ever another command so obeyed? For century after century this action has been done… in every conceivable human circumstance… from the pinnacles of earthly greatness to the refuge of fugitives in the caves and dens of the earth… for kings at their crowning and for criminals going to the scaffold.
GREGORY DIX

Guidelines

During this week we have explored a little of the Bible's theology of worship, and in particular we have explored some connections between worship and mission. We have been reminded of the capacity of creation to worship its creator, and of the human responsibility to emancipate rather than smother that worship. We have seen how mission is a means to an end, while worship is an end in itself. We have glimpsed the need to root our worship in a fresh realization of who our God really is and what he has done for us. Finally we have seen the importance of freedom and order in our corporate worship life, and the centrality of the Lord's Supper to any dynamic understanding of how worship forms and develops our relationship with God.

The aims of our second week of studies will be, first of all, to continue to unpack a biblical theology of worship, and also to explore more practical means by which the church, in its worship, can not only honour God but can also capture the imaginations of churchgoers and outsiders alike.

For now, though, we finish our week with some words inspired by one of the most famous passages in the scriptures. While the form of the apostle's words in 1 Corinthians 12 is retained, the content is changed by Bishop Tom Wright, to become a reflection on the prime importance of worship:

Worship will never end; whether there be buildings, they will crumble; whether there be committees, they will fall asleep; whether there be budgets, they will add up to nothing. For we build for the present age, we discuss for the present age, and we pay for the present age; but when the age to come is here, the present age will be done away. For now we see the beauty of God through a glass, darkly, but then face to face; now we appreciate only part, but then we shall affirm and appreciate God, even as the living God has affirmed and appreciated us. So now our tasks are worship, mission and management, these three; but the greatest of these is worship.

The sacrifice of praise

1 Worship in the real world

Psalm 137

Part of the great danger in reflecting God's image back to him in worship is that we can be tempted to do so in ways that make us neglect the importance of reflecting his image out towards others. When we divorce worship and mission in this way, or we over-emphasize the 'now' of God's kingdom and forget the painful 'not yet' of our broken world, then it is no surprise that our worship will seem vacuous to God and even flippant to those outsiders or spiritual eavesdroppers who take notice of what the church is doing.

The people of Judah found it painful, impossible even, to sing 'the Lord's song' while in exile in a 'foreign land'. But that is exactly what we as the church are called to do: to worship God precisely now, precisely while the world is still in a mess, in order to show that God's kingdom is indeed the ultimate reality, and that sin and evil will not have the final word.

Here are two quotations that help us get a better grasp on the importance of worshipping the real God, from our context in the real world.

The problem with a hymnody that focuses on equilibrium, coherence, and symmetry... is that it may deceive and cover over. Life is not like that. Life is also savagely marked by disequilibrium, incoherence, and unrelieved asymmetry.

WALTER BRUEGGEMANN

Hope without honesty slides into sentimentalism. To our shame, much so-called 'Christian music' has degenerated into a nice, inoffensive, superficial Kitsch which seems blind to the pain of the world... Often I have been uplifted and inspired by the songs of the renewal movement, but, as I see it, too many betray an 'atrocious harmlessness' which sadly lags behind the movement's increasing concern for contemporary social problems. Remarkably few songs deal with the common human experiences of failure, rejection, abandonment, protest and alienation... And frequently the music too transmits a message of joy without tears, glory without suffering, resurrection without crucifixion.

JEREMY BEGBIE

2 Transfiguring creation

1 Chronicles 29:10–22a

We have seen how the 'sacrifice of praise' involves, at the deepest level, the whole of life; we have acknowledged that worship and mission are ultimately inseparable; and we have seen how, in the sacrament of bread and wine, the offering to God of all that is already his finds its supreme focus. But, within the corporate worshipping life of the local church, there are many other examples of how the raw materials of creation can and should be taken up and channelled in such a way that they might become, as it were, more articulate in praising God.

Certainly the cheerful giving of material resources is often the indispensable counterpart to creative inspiration, and the elliptical prayer of King David in 1 Chronicles 29:14—'All things come from you, and of your own have we given you'—refers to the material offerings that made possible the building of the first temple in Jerusalem. But having been given by God, and then set aside by humans for his glory, the ellipse is complete only in the transfiguration of created resources by those human beings themselves. This is all part of what it means not only for humans to worship God, but also for us to give voice to the praises of all creation.

Let's take music as one example. It is both a cultural phenomenon with its origin in man (see Jubal in Genesis 4:21), and a gift from God as acknowledged by the Sons of Korah: 'Singers and dancers alike say, "all my springs are in you"' (Psalm 87:7). Even though it took the Christian church many centuries to accept that 'lifeless instruments' could bring glory to God, the book of Psalms has no such reservations, extolling the use of many different man-made musical instruments (see Psalm 150).

Whether in singing, building cathedrals, or arranging flowers, we do not simply give the world back to God as we find it; rather we are called into partnership with God in transforming the stuff of this world to his greater glory.

3 Any place for a theology of place?

John 4:1–26

What does it mean to describe somewhere as 'a place of worship'? Simply that Christians gather there to worship, and there happens to be a roof to keep out the rain? Or can there be more to the idea of place than that?

Certainly we do well to remember that the word 'church' is never applied to a building in the New Testament, and that the body of believers themselves constitutes the living temple of the Holy Spirit (1 Corinthians 6:19; 1 Peter 2:5). In John 4, Jesus appears to be arguing that authentic worship—worship 'in spirit and in truth'—has little to do with place. Who and what and why are greater than where.

Yet, here in the context of John's Gospel, we must be careful. John loves to explore both sides of most equations, even if from our perspective the truth ends up seeming paradoxical. Indeed, elsewhere he is keen to stress the importance of place, through the narrative importance of Jesus' pilgrimages to Jerusalem.

This tension is rooted in a larger one. On one hand, John is keen to affirm his Greek audience in the notion that God and the world are infinitely different, as different as darkness and light. Yet, on the other, he is at pains to challenge his audience with a God who becomes flesh (1:14) and thereby saves rather than scraps the world.

41

So what does this theology of incarnation tell us about how we can view the places where we worship? On one hand, we are forced to acknowledge that in Christ the *whole* creation is God's holy land. As William Cowper wrote:

> Jesus, where'er thy people meet,
> There they behold thy mercy seat.
> Where'er they seek thee thou art found,
> And every place is hallow'd ground.

Yet, on the other hand, speaking of 'holy places', and even going on pilgrimage, need not have the effect of undermining the holiness of all creation, any more than prayer is to be seen as a merely human 'work' that undermines God's providence or his primary gracious presence with us. Indeed, we actually underline and signify the extent of God's love for the whole world when we acknowledge the universal in the particular. In one sense, there is nothing more special about one place than another, nothing to distinguish Calvary from Clapham Junction; but since, through Christ's incarnation, human life and work are taken up and transformed, events and human actions and habits can and do make particular places 'holy' while others may never be consciously ascribed that tag.

4 Singing and music in corporate worship

Colossians 3:12–17

The power of music on the human mind is undisputed. It can calm the angry, light up the face of the child with the severest learning difficulties, tap the memories of the Alzheimer's patient, and be the 'food of love' that sets the pulse racing. Because this, like all power, can sometimes be mis-used, many Christians down the years have been highly suspicious of music. But the Bible is clear that its power can and should be harnessed for the benefit of the church and the glory of God. As Christopher Smart put it so succinctly, 'Glorious the song, when God's the theme.'

As Paul encourages the church at Colossae to submit to God's word and to love one another, he speaks in particular of congregational singing as an integral part of church life. And, however much the Psalms may imply an encouragement to the invention of musical instruments (each transfiguring created sound in their own particular way), it is the innate instrument of the human voice that Paul wants to highlight here. As the early church continued to obey Paul's injunction, it did so for broadly two reasons.

First, it is something that the whole congregation can join in. Of course there is a gifting and a need for worship leading, just as for any gift of the Spirit; and whether the leaders are robed choirs or worship bands, it is important for a congregation not to undermine or resent the gifting of others. But corporate worship is, by definition, something for the whole people of God, the 'one body', not only for the élite. In the words of David Hustad, 'Somehow, about forty per cent of churchgoers seem to have picked up the idea that "singing in churches is for singers". The truth is that "singing is for believers". The relevant question is not "Do you have a voice?" but, "Do you have a song?"'

Second, as Augustine famously said, 'to sing is to pray twice'. Music is not a magical key into the presence of God, but neither is it a mere package for the words. Certainly the way a composer sets a text can help us to grasp the meaning of that text better, and rhythm and melody even help us to memorize the truth articulated by the words (it is no coincidence that the creeds are written in a hymnic form). But music itself is about more than this. From Bach to Björk, the structure and manipulation of sounds can themselves point us to spatial and temporal dimensions of the gospel.

On day one of this week, we touched on this when we explored the importance of reflecting both the perfection of God and also the pain and honesty of the real world. How a composer or songwriter combines sounds and moves from one to another, using both harmony and dissonance, will say a lot about his or her view of God and the world, at conscious and unconscious levels.

5 Getting used to holistic worship

Revelation 5

An old 'high church' jibe towards 'low church' colleagues and friends came as follows: 'There are only two smells after death—sulphur and incense— so you'd better start getting used to one of them now!' And certainly we read of incense filling the heavenly throne room in Revelation 5.

The counter-argument has tended to emphasize the dangers of religiosity and even idolatry that can follow from fussy or complex liturgical trappings. Heavenly worship should not be, cannot be, contained within human frameworks. If we try to lock worship within a 'cage of gold', a man-made prison of religion, we find that in fact we have destroyed it, and are left with nothing.

The point is well made, but if the use of colour and sound and smell and gesture in our corporate worship can run the risk of become heartless 'ritualism', then throwing all this out in favour of a suit and tie and a whitewashed wall can perhaps betray an undercooked theology of creation and incarnation.

Because the Lamb has taken on flesh and shed his blood to redeem the physical world, our worship too ought to be 'embodied', not in order to worship material things, but in order to offer them back to the creator.

The youth minister at a church I once knew took a group of eight-year-olds to a cathedral for the day. At the end of the afternoon they had a spare half-hour, during which the youth minister felt sure they would all head off to the shop for ice-cream and souvenirs. In fact, all they wanted to do was to revisit the stillness of the crypt in order to light candles and fill in prayer cards. The minister told me this story, and then said, 'Oh well, they'll grow out of it.' Not if they are encouraged to read the Bible!

6 The fellowship of the Holy Spirit

Acts 2:42–47

Some years ago, the *Church Times* included as its weekly cartoon a picture of a burnt-out church in ruins. The roof had gone, the walls were smouldering, and the whole place looked like a battle zone. Behind the pews crouched well-armed rival groups of demure old ladies, and the caption ran, 'For a while the argument seemed to favour the *New English Hymnal*.'

Unfortunately this is not far from the truth. We have already seen in our readings from Romans and Colossians the need for love, kindness and compassion as prerequisites to acceptable worship, and in Matthew 5:23–24 Jesus warns us of the need to be reconciled to one another before we offer any sacrifice to God. But so often we are drawn into what Marva Dawn calls 'worship wars' that mistake issues of emphasis and taste for the substance of the gospel. By contrast, Acts 2 models for us a church that knows its priorities—the love and communion of the Holy Spirit.

Of course, having 'everything in common' does not mean there is no room for debate and disagreement, but it does mean challenging some of our church subcultures, where individualisms and party agendas are allowed to distract us from those important battles that are worth fighting. As we seek to please God and to connect with the imagination of those who come through our church doors, regularly and occasionally, we need more than ever to know what those key battles are, and to fight even those in a way that does not undermine the very worship we seek to offer.

Guidelines

5/2

As we conclude our series of studies on the theme of worship, it is time to spell out the major realities that underpin some of the theological and practical areas we have been exploring. The first is the cross and resurrection of Jesus. All our worship is Paschal worship—taking place only in the power of Christ's triumph over death and evil. This is the singular victory that opens up our relationship with God and restores his image within us. Christ's death and resurrection enable us to sing 'the Lord's song' even though we must take account of the 'foreign land' in which we still dwell. The cross and resurrection are the paradigm and the trigger for that transfiguration of all creation, a transfiguration in which we are called to take our part. They are the guarantee of God's commitment to redeem, not replace, his good creation—and are thus our chief encouragement to use the colours and sounds of creation as part of our offering of praise and thanksgiving.

The second underpinning reality is the doctrine of the Trinity. The fellowship and love that lie at the heart of God's own being are the cause and model for the church's own corporate life, a life ultimately of harmony and not division. The doctrine of the Trinity teaches us the severe limits of hierarchical structures, and instead opens the way for all members of the church, equipped with the 'voice' of their gifts, to praise and worship. The Trinity stands as our supreme warning against forget-ting the importance of either unity or diversity in any aspect of church life, not least the expression of our commitment and love for God through worship.

45

And so we end where we began, with a consideration of just how it is that we are enabled to worship, not only for the good of ourselves but the good of the world.

With reference to a passage in the epistles that we have so far left aside, the musician and theologian Jeremy Begbie writes:

We are never more truly 'priests of creation' than when we are made one with Christ through the Spirit, when the one true High Priest makes us priests with Him. For it is in Him that creation has been re-ordered towards God, and through Him that as God's people we can be rightly related to the natural world. At the profoundest level, it is only as we are in Christ that we will be able to discern aright the latent order of creation (and not misread its disorder), develop it and redeem it... For Christ, the true High Priest, for whom and by whom all things exist, is the one who stands in our midst, leading us in our worship of the Creator: 'I will proclaim thy name to my brethren, in the midst of the congregation I will praise thee' (Hebrews 2:12). (RSV).

FURTHER READING

Jeremy Begbie, *Music in God's Purposes*, Handsel Press, 1989.

Marva Dawn, *Reaching Out, Without Dumbing Down: A theology of worship for the turn-of-the-century culture*, Eerdmans, 1995.

John Drane, *The McDonaldisation of the Church*, DLT, 2000.

Evelyn Underhill, *Worship* (revised edition), Eagle, 1991.

Tom Wright, *For All God's Worth*, Triangle, 1997.

AMOS FOR TODAY

Reading the prophets often leaves us with the problem of moving from 'there and then' to 'here and now'. The traditional method of drawing parallels with today and then suggesting morals and lines of action is not altogether satisfactory because we know so little of what life was like then, which means that 'parallels' may not be parallel at all. Even if they are, our world is so totally different as to limit their usefulness severely.

After working with Christians in Latin America, a biblical scholar, Carroll R, suggests that in the case of Amos we should aim at 'a poetic reading within a rich understanding of the cultural context in which it is to be interpreted'. In other words, beginning with our own culture and situation, we treat the text as poetry, accepting the anonymity of the characters but pausing to ponder words and concepts that have a local or contemporary resonance.

To help the process, we can explore what Brueggemann calls 'a zone of imagination' which stands between the input of the text and the outcome of attitudes, belief or behaviour. This is an intensely personal area, full of 'baggage' based on what we have always been told—a mix of powerful interests, deep fears and unresolved hurts—but, if we give freedom to the text and our imagination, we may well find that the Bible comes alive in a new way. Seeds that we did not even know were there may begin to shoot and blossom.

In the first week, try to hear what Amos is saying, and ask yourself what might have led him to say it. See if you find yourself suddenly appearing 'in the frame'. In the second week, as we revisit some of the territory, use your imagination to see what meaning his words might have for us.

Quotations are taken from the New Revised Standard Version.

1 Ecology is a human problem / 6/2

Amos 1:1–10

Think of Amos as a layman, a provincial (Tekoa is about eight miles from Jerusalem), and probably more of a sheep-dealer than a shepherd, with his feet firmly on the ground, well aware of the importance of relating to the natural order and not unaware of the economic implications.

Verse 2 takes us to a world of ecological anxieties and natural disasters. There is a food shortage and a drought. People are naturally starting to ask, 'What have we done wrong?' or 'Why are we being punished?' Use your imagination to think who are likely to be the main sufferers and who might seize the opportunity to turn circumstances to their own advantage. Some will be handy with 'explanations', some ready to play on people's guilt. Then ask yourself a different question. What do we have to do to put things right?

Ecological problems need ecological answers before they need theological theories. In times of crisis, action and scientific know-how come before theory. What theology can do, however, is to create an atmosphere of unity and co-operation to help and to find answers. It is a time to bury the hatchet and tackle the job in hand. Rival groups can stand shoulder to shoulder; natural competitors can begin to work together; nations can set up joint lines of communication; different faiths can address everything that is not specifically a faith issue together. Who knows? Such co-operation might prove to be not only a sensible, creative and effective way of dealing with the problem, but also a means of discovering 'the other' in a new way.

Too often, what happens is something quite different. Damascus would rather thrash people than thresh corn (v. 3). Weapons for war come before tools for agriculture, and national security before social security, bringing destruction on themselves as well as on their enemies. Tyre, on the other hand, is busy uprooting and moving whole populations (v. 9), leading to forced labour, potential slavery and prostitution —not only for their enemies but even for their own kith and kin.

Prayer: Father, keep me ever mindful of the needs of others in times of crisis, ever sensitive to the natural order, and a tough critic of 'Damascus' and 'Tyre'.

2 Victims of wrath

Amos 1:11–15

The dearth of detail in these verses enables us to identify the underlying issues: how we treat people, and how we so easily slip into situations where we dehumanize them.

In Edom, a man lifts his sword against his own brother (v. 11; shades of Jacob and Esau fighting in the womb), which suggests family breakdown. Another possibility is that 'brother' means kinsman, in the sense of relationships within the clan—so perhaps we are to think of civil war or ethnic cleansing. If our world is a global village, then every man is our brother, every woman our sister, every person our kinsman.

So how do people get themselves into this state? Presumably few of the Ammonites ever had such hatred of pregnant women that they derived personal satisfaction from disembowelling them (v. 13). Perhaps we can envisage two other possibilities. One is that the problem started with a bit of antipathy, leading to acrimony, which, in the face of some resistance, became physical violence; and before they knew what they were doing, it had all got out of control. The other is that the perpetrators were simply under pressure, possibly under orders; and those in charge had a very different agenda, with no intention of doing the dirty work themselves.

The word of God may become clearer if we look at ourselves. Rape and ill-treatment of pregnant women is not unknown in our world, but there are many more subtle ways of dehumanizing people, such as alienation, misrepresentation, exploitation and unhealthy competition, backed by a policy of 'might is right' and aided and abetted by all kinds of economic handouts and sweeteners. The result is the same—hurt, anger, sorrow and regret, themselves all further forms of punishment and dehumanization which seem to require nobody to administer them.

Recognizing such situations, trying to understand what is going on and where it may lead by entering into the experience of victims, may be a much more effective way of responding to Amos' words than simply lining up behind him in condemnation.

Prayer: Father, help me to recognize anger in myself and in others long before it gets out of control. Give me the wisdom and strength to overcome it or to channel it into something more positive and closer to love.

3 Institutionalized abuse

8/2

Amos 2:1–8

Long before Christian morality, the Jews had some fairly clear ideas about what we now associate with 'human rights'. Amos identifies abuse of power at three possible points: people, law and religion.

In Moab, it's people. What they did would be regarded as sacrilege in most communities (v. 1). In the ancient Near East, defilement of a corpse or tomb was regarded with horror, and it was not uncommon to find, inscribed on tombs or coffins, curses on anyone who disturbed their contents. Burning bones in this way would be unthinkable. But is there more to it than mass graves and violation of cemeteries? What about the violation of human rights leading to abuse of people who are still living?

Judah's offence is the abuse of the law (v. 4). Moab might be forgiven on the grounds that 'people like that know no better'. Judah did know better: they had the law, but they weren't keeping it. Nobody ever does, not in every detail, but these people were positively rejecting it—like rulers who think they are above the law and can get away with anything, sometimes by rejecting it outright and sometimes by clever little twists, so that they can claim to keep the letter when flouting the spirit of it. If this can happen within a single nation, think how much more difficult things become when we get to the UN or international law and agreements.

In Israel's case, they were abusing religion. They had forgotten that they were once slaves in Egypt and that their faith required them always to pay due respect to the under-privileged—the poor, the needy, the diseased and the afflicted; to people in debt (v. 6); and to women (v. 7), whether they be sister or daughter, a maid or one of the temple prostitutes. This is not just about what goes on in the office or the factory, but among 'the faithful', where such abuse is even more reprehensible and its effects often far more damaging. The issue is not 'who' or 'where', but what our actions say about our attitude to people.

Prayer: Father, before I let loose all my feelings about institutionalized abuse, keep me focused on the victims. Is there something I can do to help even one?

4 Take a look at your lifestyle

Amos 3

There are some moments in life that we find utterly incomprehensible. We say things like, 'I just don't believe it' or, 'I thought I was seeing things' or, 'I thought, it can't be happening to me.' They happen in many ways. A perfectly healthy person who has never consulted a doctor suddenly has a stroke or a heart attack in late mid-life; one of our 'heroes' falls from grace; we are let down or openly taken to pieces by our best friend. This is how the people of Israel felt when Amos turned his guns on them. All the surrounding nations were fair game for his attacks if that was what he wanted to do—most of them probably deserved it—'but not me. I'm special… different… always have been.' 'No,' says Amos; 'you too.'

But why? Suppose you have been let down by your friend. You must have been party to the friendship and there must have been years of understanding between you. So what can have happened to bring about this disappointment? Start with yourself, not with your friend. Things don't happen without a cause. If your friend is suddenly making a big noise, there must be something to make a big noise about. If you feel trapped, there must have been a trap, so who set it and why? Instead of just reacting, blaming the messenger or being content with the last cause in the chain, dig deeper. Use the situation as an opportunity to examine your own lifestyle, to see if there is any way you might have contributed to it.

Having got so far, the next thing to do is to pull yourself together. It need not be the end of the world. Friendships can recover and be rebuilt. People can pick themselves up from the direst of tragedies and live again. There is always some hope to cling to with a God who hopes in spite of hopelessness, much as a shepherd finds hope in the face of death when he rescues an ear or a couple of legs (v. 12)—or as a mother who has lost her baby clings to a few items of the baby's clothing because it helps her to move on to the future. Only those who refuse to listen, to learn from their experience and change their ways are doomed to total destruction —and that is their choice.

Prayer: Thank you, God, for your mercy and your patience. Let me never take them for granted, and help me to offer them to others.

5 God in my image

This picture (or poem?) is fairly specific. The fertile land east of Galilee produced a race of cattle that were sleek and fat, not unlike the women who were living well on the money-making activities and heartless exploitative practices of their husbands—perhaps better translated 'lords' to bring out the contrast between what the 'lords' were doing and what the Lord had said. The idea seems to be that they were never satisfied, always demanding more of this, more of that.

To avoid sexism, think of bulls as well as cows. Or bring to mind the commercial world with its eye on ever-increasing profits, the unstoppable thrust to raise the standard of living, not least for those who already have most—more choice, bigger and better schools, hospitals and services, and instant litigation if 'my share' is found wanting. Throw in all the new, improved gadgets and gizmos and you may see verse 1 as a fair reflection of contemporary society, and all without much thought about the price to be paid and who will pay it.

We could relate Amos' picture to an increasing interest in religion, sometimes referred to as 'spirituality'—not the kind that demands long-term commitment, regular duties, sacrifices, social justice and a concern for others, but the kind that prefers to place flowers at the scene of every accident and multiply moments of silence to remember past events, always capable of pulling out loose cash for the latest disaster and never missing church at Christmas or Easter.

Amos focuses on the incongruity. 'If that's what you want,' he seems to say, 'get on with it. Pay your dues; go through all the rituals. But just check whether you are worshipping at the right shrine. Bethel and Gilgal have nothing to offer you: your forebears committed you to someone and something different. Check that you are not 'using religion' to validate your own values, creating a new religion that offers cheap grace while you reconstruct God in your own image.

Prayer: Father, restore to me an understanding of your word in all its breadth. Let me blink once and take a fresh look at so much around me that I take for granted. Let me blink twice and see what I have been missing.

6 What is God trying to tell us?

Amos 4:6–12

God ponders on his own problem. What does he have to do to get through to these people?

Imagine that you live in a land where, one year, there was no harvest—literally, none. Consider the implications in detail. What would you miss most? What would you eat? What would be the consequences for your health? And what would be the consequential effects on the economy, industry, transport, and so on?

The following year, things are a little better and the outlook more hopeful—until, that is, the mildew strikes and the locusts swarm in and devour everything. Now what are the consequences, and how do you feel about them?

The third year, people are dying like flies, of disease. The neighbourhood is increasingly unpleasant to live in, and although there are still a few good things around—remnants of past glories—nobody has much interest in them any more. There are more important things to worry about. Neighbouring countries are aware of your predicament. Your nation is an ideal candidate for asset-stripping raids from over the border, and when your young men try to defend what you have left, they are quickly routed and put to the sword.

What questions would you be asking? 'What have we done to deserve this? Why is God behaving like this? If he is a God of love, why doesn't he stop it?' Try asking a different question: 'Is somebody trying to tell us something?' Amos has no doubt. God is trying to tell us to come to our

53

senses and to come to terms with reality. But in such a tough situation, what might reality be? And how would we get there?

Prayer: Father God, if reality is coming to terms with you and the world in which I find myself, help me to see it as you would wish it to be. Then give me strength to do whatever I can to move in that direction, in the small circle where I have any influence.

Guidelines

Here are some suggestions for developing what you have gained from this week's reading.

- Choose one 'poem' by Amos which touches a nerve more than the others do. Relate it to one similar situation in your own experience and then try writing (in prose) what you think Amos might say.
- Choose one 'problem' you are living with, to which Amos alludes. Imagine Amos with you in the room and have an imaginary conversation. What would you say to him? How might he reply?
- Make a list of the points of tension between the demands of ecology and the creation of a stable economy. How do you think Amos might handle them?
- Start a discussion on the differences between the traditional religious rituals of yesterday (worship, sacraments, saints' days and so on) and popular folk religion today. Do you think Amos would see any differences between the two? If so, what might they be?

1 The beginnings of hope

Amos 5:1–17

After all the tough talk, Amos begins a reconstruction. If things are as bad as he says, what can these people hope for? What can they do? Well, how about a change of attitude?

The first step is a recognition of where they are—no excuses; no special pleading. Hope springs not from blind Panglossian optimism but from realism. But this is not the same as saying, 'Things will have to get worse before they get better.' The first sign of hope is when you can see 1000 men going to war and 900 body bags coming back, and say, 'All right, I agree. Something has gone drastically wrong.'

The next step is to avoid the temptation to escape to Bethel and Gilgal yet again. They may be the traditional watering-places of yesteryear for people who wanted to 'seek the Lord', but for Amos they are simply old-fashioned folk religion. They are a return to the old habits, from the time before they embraced the new revelation with its fresh opportunities. Amos sees them as an escape. 'Leave them alone,' is his wisdom. 'They are doomed. Better to start somewhere else' (v. 5). When the Quakers rejected traditional forms of worship, including the sacraments, in favour of silence, it was because they wanted to start in another place. They wanted to find God everywhere. Everything would be holy; every meal would be a sacrament. It may not be the whole gospel but at least it was an attempt to get back to first principles and concentrate on something that had been lost—something in which everybody could be engaged.

For Amos and his generation, the new start from first principles meant learning to surrender all the security that they had built around themselves (houses of stone) at the expense of other people, and the artificial structures they had created to insulate themselves from the hazards of living (pleasant vineyards). Sadly, verses 16–17 give little grounds for hope that anybody listened.

Prayer: Father, keep me always sensitive to the simple difference between good and evil, between loving my fellow human beings and being indifferent to them.

2 Prayer versus social justice

Amos 5:18–24

Imagine soldiers going into battle and simply praying that enemy bullets would not find them, or others going to church to pray for deliverance from the horrors and disasters they are always reading about in the papers. Some churches flourish on the back of a spirituality that offers an escape from the toils and tribulations of daily life. In varying ways, all are saying, 'Surely the Lord is with us and will help us.'

Amos courts unpopularity (a good sign of a true prophet) when he says (in effect), 'Not a bit of it. Forget your sacrifices, offerings, sacred rites and rituals. I am not even listening.' Then he concludes, 'Let justice flow on like a river and righteousness like a never-failing torrent' (v. 24, REB). Why does he say this? Because he believes that this popular image of God and religion is a delusion. It is a tough message for a religious figure to deliver, but the truth must be told.

If you heard Amos' message today, whether from a religious leader, a parish priest or lay person, in church or on the street corner, how would you react? Would you say, 'This man is crazy and seems set on destroying everything the faith has stood for?' 'This man is not against true worship but false worship?' 'This is a justifiable tirade against popular religious behaviour rather than the real thing?' Your answer will tell you quite a bit about how you see worship and how you feel about people who worship in different ways from yours.

But suppose the message is not about worship. Perhaps the underlying question is how we think of ourselves as 'seeking the Lord' and how we know when he is with us. In that case, it is not about people worshipping in the wrong way or the wrong place—Bethel and Gilgal; Orthodox, Catholic or Protestant. It is about our failure to realize that 'seeking the Lord' means taking a public stand against evil and exploitation wherever we find it. It's about finding him 'in the throng and press'. The formula is not prayer (or worship) versus social justice, but the realization that social justice can be prayer and that those who engage in it will find God.

Prayer: Recall a moment when you fought a battle for truth or justice, and the feeling of satisfaction that it gave you. Give thanks to God for the realization of his presence.

3 Indifference, the opposite of love

Amos 6

Think of a church (or other institution) where everything is going well. There are no membership problems: people are queuing up to join. No skills shortage: they have specialists to handle every kind of emergency. No serious problems that can't be sorted out either by reference to the right person or by a quick word of prayer. Bible study? Everybody comes. A personal crisis? Everybody rallies round.

Now focus on a situation of tragedy or disaster—not one of the big ones for the Disasters Emergency Committee, but a delicate case of injustice, which most people would prefer not to know about. If you were to challenge that problem-free institution with the situation, which of the following responses would you expect?

- There will always be people like that.
- Sad, but there's nothing we can do about it.
- It's not our business—more a matter for the social services, the courts or the politicians.
- Great—get them to come along and we will care for them and pray for them.

Where, then, do you locate the people Amos had in mind when he talked about those who were lying on beds of ivory, lounging on couches, helping themselves to food, enjoying wine and so on, while remaining quite insensitive to the ruins around them (vv. 4–6)?

The sins to look for are a false sense of security, excessive self-indulgence and callous indifference to others, especially among those who might be regarded as leaders or trendsetters but who are unlikely to be moved if the world collapsed round their ears. Once identified, concentrate on the sins rather than the offenders, noting the difference in detail from the time of Amos, but concentrating on the underlying offence of self-centredness and indifference, which is symptomatic of a wider attitude affecting other walks of life.

Prayer: Father in my concern for the victims of injustice, make me ever mindful of the injustice resulting from indifference, and not only the indifference of other people but mine as well.

4 The struggle to hope

Here we have the first three of five visions. Amos struggles to find a ray of hope. The locusts threatened, but were not as disastrous as they first appeared (vv. 1–3). Then there was a fire eating up the land, but it stopped short of total destruction (vv. 4–6). In both cases, deliverance seemed like an answer to prayer. In the first, there was the possibility of natural healing and recovery. In the second, what the fire had consumed was gone, but something had been left. Then comes the plumbline (vv. 7–9).

There are translation problems here, and we don't have space to go into details. There is no evidence that the Hebrews ever had anything like a plumbline. 'Tin' nowadays is the preferred equivalent. With bronze, it made weapons of destruction, and the Assyrians were using it. So we might envisage God standing on a wall with his unconquerable weapons ready to strike. Surely from this there can be no escape.

To appreciate the force of this vision, try to enter into the emotions of a man who has faced death twice (perhaps with a life-threatening illness and an operation) and come through miraculously, but just when he is beginning to look forward, a third attack threatens, far more potentially damaging than the other two. How can he go on hoping? It is the mood of a nation threatened for years by an enemy, twice having seen them off, and then finding them once more at the gates begging for blood. Or think of a marriage that has gone through the same experience, or parents whose child has run away and come back twice, but this time may not return at all.

This is the moment when there is no answer. In the first two visions, Amos pleaded (successfully) with God, but this time there isn't even a request. Things are so bad, it isn't even worth trying. Imagine Amos simply picking up his bags, heaving a sigh of grief and setting off home, muttering, 'I sometimes wonder why I bother.' It is the cry of dereliction. There are times when there is no hope—but those are the moments when we have to go on hoping.

Prayer: Father, when there is no hope and I don't even have the desire, never mind the will, to do anything about it, give me strength simply to hang on and believe that one day the light will shine again.

5 Nobody listens

/12/2

The next vision is a basket of summer fruit. In the Hebrew, this is a play on words, with sound suggesting sense. The basic letters are *qz*. If you say the word one way, you get 'summer fruit', but say it another way and it means 'end'. Amos has obviously not recovered from his loss of hope, and we can attribute his mood to the fact that whatever he says, and however many times he says it, nobody seems to listen. Most readers will know how he felt.

Worse still, not only have the people of Israel failed to respond to Amos, they have failed miserably to learn from their own experience. They are still trampling on the poor, with offences that have an incredibly modern ring about them. They are so keen to get back to making money, they can't wait for the end of the religious festivals. Religion must never get in the way of business. They prefer to adjust sizes, weights and measures so as to sell less—adjust exchange rates and increase prices. With no Standards Officer, scales could soon be rigged, and often were. With computers, they could have confused people even more, with rapid changes of prices, contents, discounts and special offers. Unemployment figures and league tables could have been slanted to their own advantage. Sawdust could have been turned into lucrative chipboard.

All the old fears—inflation, interest rates, exchange rates and a stop-go economy—are back. Doesn't it make you quake? Are we all going to be knocked from pillar to post yet again? Perhaps one day we will wake up, but unless it is soon it may be too late.

Not that it's exactly like last time. Some things have changed. The problem is slightly different. Once it was a shortage of food, and people resorted to violence because they had nothing to eat. The country had no resources. Now there are resources, although they are quickly grabbed by a few who will always find ways of exploiting them for their own benefit, unless they are controlled. This is not a famine of wheat and bread. It is a famine of truth and justice—that is, the word of the Lord.

Prayer: Father, keep me humble, uncomplaining and non-judgmental. Help me to think hard about what I have, to visualize those who have not; and then give me the urge to share wherever I can.

6 The remnant

If things go on as they are, Amos can see only destruction following in their wake. This is a world of no escape, neither in the heights nor in the depths, neither on land nor on sea (vv. 2–3). He feels that he has a sixth sense, rather like some of our scientists who make their forecasts and forebodings about global warming, ecological disaster, carbon dioxide emissions and so on with a tale of woe stretching into the next millennium. Over such events, we know we have little control. Amos has no doubt that God does have control. Try to identify times when you have felt exactly as he did, but not always with the same conviction about God.

Only in the closing verses does the mood change, when Amos pumps out a message of hope with more conviction than he has shown in all his poetry so far. The good old days (as in the time of David) will return. Ruined cities will be rebuilt. Agriculture will be falling over itself with successful crops. The hills will be lush with wine. People who work and produce will enjoy the products of their labour. They will live in the cities they build instead of building cities for other people. They will drink the wine from their own vineyards and eat the produce from their own gardens. At its heart, this is a picture of a God who can never give up on his creation, which is the message that all those who have shared the experiences of Amos, in every generation, want to hear.

At the same time, it leaves us with a choice. We can read it simply as a picture of the faithful remnant, once all the sinners have been dealt with and only the faithful remain (vv. 9–10). Alternatively, we can see it as a vision of what is likely to happen even though everything always seems to point in the opposite direction, and even though it is difficult, particularly at certain times, to see how it could ever happen. Which interpretation do you want to believe? Your answer may not tell you much about what is, or will be, but it will tell you a lot about yourself.

Prayer: Thank you, Father, for that vision. Now help me to interpret it and work out where I fit.

Guidelines

Here are some suggestions for developing what you have gained from this week's reading.

- Read Amos 5:14–15, and compare Micah 6:8; Deuteronomy 6:4–5; Leviticus 19:18 and Luke 10:27. If this is the core of Judaism and Christianity, what else do we need? Without reference to the traditions, make a list of not more than five things that you would be looking for. Invite your friends to do the same and exchange ideas.
- Work out the wider implications of the sins of omission and indifference in your own society.
- Count the number of times Amos seems to strike hope and then lose it. What do you think was going on in his mind to cause his mixed feelings? Think of someone going through the same experience, or a time when you went through it yourself. Were the causes the same or different?
- Clarify some differences between traditional Christian faith as you grew up with it, and more popular current folk religion. To what extent can you identify folk religion with what Amos regarded as the paganism of Bethel and Gilgal?

FURTHER READING

A.G. Auld, *Amos* (Old Testament Guides), Sheffield Academic Press, 1995.

R.J. Coggins, *Joel and Amos* (New Century Bible Commentary), Sheffield Academic Press, 2000.

Walter Brueggemann, *The Bible and Postmodern Imagination*, SCM Press, 1993 (chapter 3 especially).

Mark Daniel Carroll R, *Contexts for Amos. Prophetic Poetics in Latin American Perspectives*, JSOT Press, 1992 (chapter 5 especially).

2 CORINTHIANS

Former Archbishop George Carey wrote of this letter by Paul, 'No book in the New Testament gives more insight into the problems of Christian ministry than 2 Corinthians.' It is also the letter that reveals Paul's heart most fully. We see him 'warts and all', at his most vulnerable in the midst of conflict from within the church. It deals, among other issues, with coping with misunderstandings, the Christian use of authority within a church, money, suffering and Christ-like spirituality. May I suggest that you read the passage slowly through twice, perhaps in two translations, then ponder it and read the notes. Next ask yourself a question such as those suggested. Then read the passage one final time and pray. These notes are based on the NIV, but any modern scholarly translation can be used.

Corinth was a great city from the seventh century BC in ancient Greece, but Rome razed it to the ground in 146BC. One hundred years later, Julius Caesar refounded it as a Roman colony. By AD50 it was flourishing as a brash, modern, trade metropolis—'a cosmopolitan boom town with shallow roots', as one writer put it. Most of its inhabitants were striving for honour through wealth and its spectacular display. Trade was its *raison d'être*. Corinth dominated both the north–south trade through Greece and, using its two ports, the east–west shipping from Italy to the eastern Mediterranean. On its lofty mountain, called Akrocorinth, stood the temple to Aphrodite, goddess of sex, encouraging all the immoral practices that went with a large port anyway.

Paul's dealings with Corinth are disputed and not easy to reconstruct in detail. They spanned seven years and at least three personal visits and four letters. In my view, our 1 Corinthians is his second letter. He wrote a previous one (see 1 Corinthians 5:9). Then came a 'severe' third letter (see 2 Corinthians 2:4; 7:8–13). The fourth letter was our 2 Corinthians. It is tempting to see parts of earlier letters within 2 Corinthians, and many do. There is no textual evidence for this, however, and it is simpler to see the sharp changes of mood within the letter as being caused by other factors. What is important for us is the relevance of this difficult letter for our churches today. May we grow to share Paul's passionate love and pastoral wisdom for this awkward bunch of Christians with all their problems.

1 God, suffering and us

2 Corinthians 1:1–11

I have written some long and difficult letters during my years as a vicar and on a theological college staff, but none of them begin to resemble Paul's second (actually his fourth) letter to the church at Corinth. The letter is mainly from Paul (Timothy features only slightly) and mainly to the church groups in Corinth, though clearly there are now other Christian groups in the Roman province of Achaia or southern Greece. Two years earlier, when Paul wrote 1 Corinthians (around AD54), it was addressed only to Corinth. New churches must have been planted since then. Troubled churches can also be growing churches!

These opening verses raise a key issue for Paul and all Christians: the spiritual importance of suffering. Suffering and 'comfort' dominate this passage: the Greek word-group for 'comfort' comes ten times in five verses. Its basic meaning is to come alongside to help, and the underlying idea is of one person being with another person in a way that changes their mood for the better. God is like that with us so that we can be like that with others (v. 4). Then comes one of Paul's big ideas. What is true of Jesus is true of his followers—the principle of interchange. Just as Jesus carried a cross, so will we (Mark 8:34). Christian leaders' suffering can also interchange and overflow into comfort to others, and so can their experience of being comforted, since their example can lead to others being better able to endure patiently (vv. 5–7).

Paul then opens his heart and tells them of something specific and life-threatening that has recently happened to him in western Turkey. One commentator wisely says that it is 'impossible to identify it with certainty'. My guess is that it was a disease that nearly killed him in Ephesus, but that God saw him through. So far it had not recurred and Paul was confident that, if it did, God would rescue him again. Even had he died, though, God raises the dead! Above all, Paul learned to rely on God as well as their prayers. The important outcome was that a lot more thanksgiving went to God (vv. 8–11).

When and how have you received comfort in a big way? Has that changed the way you relate to others?

How do you react to the idea that Paul almost despaired of life? What enabled him, and what enables you, not to give up?

2 The 'can't win' syndrome

2 Corinthians 1:12—2:4

Sometimes, usually when relationships are poor, whatever you do or say is misunderstood. Paul here was in such a 'can't win' situation, and he did not have a phone or e-mail with which to sort things out quickly. He had told the Corinthians that he would visit them again, stay the coming winter (probably AD54) and then come a second time after seeing the Macedonian churches en route to Judea (v. 16; see 1 Corinthians 16:5). However, he brought the first visit forward and shortened it a lot. It became known as the 'painful' visit (2:1). Because of this, Paul cancelled the second visit and wrote the 'severe' letter (2:3–4). It was his third letter to them and is probably lost, although some people think that 2 Corinthians 10—13 is part of it. Some at Corinth, because of the change of plans, called him fickle and untrustworthy (v. 17).

In reply, Paul makes two major points. First, the Father, the Lord Jesus Christ and the Spirit as Paul preached them are all utterly reliable and to be trusted (vv. 18–22). Jesus embodies this reliability, fulfilling all God's promises through Israel's history. The very word 'Amen', which Christians said to endorse a prayer, is spoken 'through Jesus' (v. 20) and means 'Yes' or 'I agree; that's true'. The word 'Christ' means 'anointed one'. So the Christian has Christ within by the Spirit, and the Spirit is like an anointing. Like a seal guaranteeing ownership, or like an advance down payment guaranteeing the rest later, is God's gift of the Spirit. So Paul's whole gospel message shouts, 'God is faithful'. Paul could hardly live the opposite.

Second, Paul explains the reasons for his change of mind (1:23—2:4). Motives can never be known except to God, so Paul first solemnly invokes God to endorse his truthfulness (v. 23). His reason was to spare them further pain and to enable them later to give him joy (2:2). This had happened (7:7–10), but it had cost Paul the writing of a letter he had cried over. Paul was a man of tears (Acts 20:36–37). This passage tells us much of Paul's emotions. Not all theologians have ink in their veins! 'Truth on fire' would summarize Paul's life and writings.

What can we do to minimize misunderstandings when relationships are fraught?

What aspects of Paul's character appeal to or puzzle you in this passage?

In what ways has God, through Christ and in the Spirit, proved utterly reliable to you?

3 Tough love   / 22/2

Discipline at home and within the church is unfashionable but essential, and so is restoration after repentance. Verses 5–11 show how it was done in Corinth, and provide valuable lessons for us. It is not easy to re-construct what exactly happened, but here is one possible scenario.

Paul had been insulted and his authority openly flouted before the whole church during the painful visit. This 'grief' (2:5), 'wrong' or 'injury' (7:12) had been inflicted probably by one of the new super-apostles (12:11) and not by a church member, since '*all*' had been grieved (v. 5). Paul then left Corinth and wrote a severe letter instead of returning in person. The church responded well: it disciplined the man. Possibly he was publicly rebuked and barred from communion. As Paul wrote, he had just heard from Titus the good news that they had taken Paul's advice and passed the 'test' (v. 9). Now Paul feels that it is time to restore the man (vv. 6, 10–11). He has repented and his sorrow is in danger of becoming excessive. Paul never felt that the sin had been mainly against him personally but more that it had damaged the church (v. 10). For his part, and in Christ's sight, Paul has forgiven him. Now, to stop Satan bringing bitterness and division, the man needs to have their love for him reaffirmed. Public reinstatement may well be in mind.

What lessons there are here! Paul is more concerned for the church than for himself. Michael B. Thompson comments, 'A leader with less security in Christ might well have been glad to see the back of such a troublemaker, but not the apostle.' Jesus' teaching in Luke 17:3 may have been in Paul's mind. Another commentator remarks, 'Christian discip-line is always intended to be remedial, never merely punitive'. Often today's churches ignore such sins, or the offender moves churches or leaves altogether.

At verse 14, Paul's thought totally switches, and remains on a different tack until 7:5. Some have thought that the intervening material is part of a different letter, but there is no textual evidence to support this, and Paul does it elsewhere too. Here Paul bursts out in praise for God's strange victory through Christ's death and resurrection. Strength through weakness indeed! Paul, God's minister, is caught up as a fellow victor in God's triumph. A Roman triumph, with its sacrificial smoke and aroma and the incense spreading ever wider, wafting death to foes and joyful life to fellow victors, is the picture (vv. 14–15). Paul's huge privilege and responsibility is to proclaim the gospel and so waft the aroma ever wider. But, unlike his self-confident and 'in-it-for-the-money' rivals at Corinth, Paul is far from sure that he is up to it.

In what circumstances is a church right to exercise discipline and how should it do so?

What is the profoundest experience of human forgiveness that you have encountered?

4 More glorious ministry, more glorious covenant

2 Corinthians 3:1–11

Writing a Curriculum Vitae is hard, but writing a letter to commend yourself for a job is harder still. Will anyone believe it? Some at Corinth virtually accused Paul of writing his own commendation. He had letters from no one else to commend him, they said. The charge hurt: he mentions it seven times in this letter. As they read 2 Corinthians, he senses that they will accuse him of self-commendation again (v. 1). Once again, he cannot win. H.L. Goudge comments, 'Self-defence is almost impossible without self-commendation. St Paul's opponents… made the former necessary and then blamed him for the latter.'

Paul wrote such letters for others, like Phoebe (Romans 16:1). The visitors to Corinth who opposed him brought their own. In a culture of itinerant wisdom teachers, this was commonplace; but why should Paul play that game? He was the Corinthians' spiritual father. They themselves were his 'letter', written not on papyrus with black ink made from charcoal, gum and water but by the Spirit of God and on to Paul's innermost being. They were the result of his ministry, and Christ was the letter's sender (vv. 2–3). People should learn what Paul was like by looking at the Corinthians. Quite a thought for church leaders!

Paul's confidence in them and competence as a minister all depend on what God has done and, supremely, on God's new covenant. The story of Moses and the first covenant begins to dominate Paul's thinking now. His ministry is more glorious even than Moses', because it is the new covenant that he is sharing (vv. 4–6). Two major contrasts are drawn out. First, Moses' covenant was temporary. Not only did the glory on his face fade (a point not made in Exodus 34:29–35, from where Paul took this part of the story); but that glory was on its way to being abolished anyway (v. 7). The new glory as far surpasses the old as the sun's brightness out-shines the moon, and it lasts (vv. 10–11). Second, the old covenant of the letter brought death and condemnation (vv. 6–7, 9), not because the law was in essence bad—quite the reverse. It was 'holy, righteous... good' and 'spiritual' (Romans 7:12, 14), but humankind could not keep it and so was condemned. As forecast in Jeremiah 31 and Ezekiel 36, under the new covenant and in Christ, men and women had the Spirit. He empowered them to keep the law and his presence was a foretaste and guarantee of the new resurrection life beyond the grave (5:5).

If a close friend wrote a letter commending you, what might it truthfully say?

What is most glorious for you about God's new covenant? Spend time praising God for it now.

24/2

5 Changed from glory into glory

2 Corinthians 3:12—4:6

'Completely open' or 'bold' (v. 12) is what Paul claims for his ministry in answer to his critics (see 1:13; 11:6), who preferred the sophisticated skills of the recently arrived new teachers at Corinth. It is 'hope'—that is, the certain future proclaimed by the new covenant—that makes Paul so straightforward. Paul then continues his exposition of Moses and the veil (Exodus 34:29–35). Paul's version is a free translation with a fair bit of interpretation added! His first main point is that when Paul is ministering, then glory (that is, God's revealed self) must be crystal clear for all to see, not like Moses with his shining face veiled.

In verse 14, Paul uses the veil in a different way to picture the failure of many Jews to accept the new covenant. Even then, in synagogues, Torah scrolls might well have been covered when being brought out to read. It is not, says Paul, that Torah is wrong, although its day is passing and its radiance fading (v. 13). The main problem is that the people's minds were made dull, as if a veil covered their hearts (vv. 14, 16). Semi-quoting Exodus 34:34, Paul says that for those who turn to the Lord (Jesus?), God (the Spirit?) removes the veil.

Then Paul explores the Spirit's work further. Broadening from his own ministry to the whole church ('and we... all', v. 18), Paul makes the extraordinary claim that our Christian life should be one long transformation by the Spirit into Christ's likeness, and that this happens as we reflect back the wonder or glory of the Lord *from one another*. We need to keep polishing our mirrors and grow in Christ by looking at the Spirit's work in each other.

Paul had many reasons for losing heart especially over Corinth, but he is especially kept going by God's mercy (4:1). He never ceased to be amazed both that God had chosen him, a persecutor, and that God had given him this ministry to the Gentiles. Tricks and cleverness were superfluous as well as wrong when he already had such a gospel (v. 2). What if some did not respond? Was Paul accused of ineffective preaching? Blame the god of this world (this is the only time Satan is called a god), blame the fact that people don't want Christ, blame my preaching, but never blame the gospel (vv. 3–4), says Paul.

Of verse 5, C.K. Barrett says, 'It would be hard to describe the Christian ministry more comprehensively in so few words.' It has been the motto of two churches I been part of. Verse 6 reflects not just Paul's conversion but his mulling over it. He links this new creation (see 5:17) to God's first creation of light (Genesis 1:3). That Jesus is the image of God, and Lord (vv. 4–6) was the heart of Paul's message.

'Changed from glory into glory': in what ways have you and your church changed in the last five years?

What does it mean for you that Jesus is the image of God, and Lord? How can you share this message?

6 Trouble: a Christ-centred perspective

2 Corinthians 4:7–18

You cannot walk over the site of any ancient city without treading on broken pieces of pottery. Clay pots were coarse and commonplace, whatever the value of their contents. Paul uses this picture to say of his ministry, 'The messenger is unimportant but the message is treasure indeed'. To validate his ministry, he could have mentioned the miracles he had done, but instead he concentrates on his troubles and God's support of him in them (vv. 7–9).

As an apostle and minister, indeed as a Christian at all, his life had to mirror his message (vv. 10–12). That gospel's foundation was Jesus' death and resurrection (1 Corinthians 15:3–5). Paul uses the personal name 'Jesus' on its own, unusually and four times in verses 10, 11 and 14. As A. Schlatter put it, 'As Jesus' herald, Paul told the story of Jesus' passion. He not only told it; he experienced it too.' That was the way to discovering a foretaste of Jesus' resurrection life as well. If we want that, we have to be prepared to see crucifixion in our lives as well. But this way, and this way only, new life comes to others too (v. 12).

Verses 13–15 develop this theme further. They start by quoting Psalm 116:10, but the whole psalm was probably in Paul's mind. It echoes gratitude to God for deliverance and the sense of wanting to share it with others. What does Paul share? To Jesus' death and resurrection, he adds Jesus' return (v. 14) and the hope that God will be glorified by more and more Corinthians (v. 15).

'We do not lose heart' (v. 16) returns to 4:1. It is worthwhile to look at the many reasons not to do so that Paul has given in verses 13–15, and chapters 3 and 4 as a whole. The final verses start the theme of Paul's growing physical frailty. 'Outwardly' he is now in his 50s and has suffered appallingly (11:23–30). His natural faculties are declining and he has had a death scare (1:8–9). But his Christ-centred perspective concentrates on the Spirit's inner renewal (3:18) and the final reality of which it is a foretaste: 'the eternal glory that far outweighs' all his troubles (v. 17). It is here that Paul, and we, should fix our gaze.

What weaknesses in your life open you up especially to God's transforming grace?

What keeps you going in your Christian life? Compare what kept Paul going.

Guidelines

2612

It is suggested that you read through the passages and questions below and meditate on one or two—perhaps reading them in a fresh translation. Next, work out your answers to the question(s). Finally, turn your reflections into prayers. An alternative method would be simply to re-read all four chapters, preferably in a different translation, and ask God to lay on your heart one or two passages or verses to ponder further.

- 'Conflict reveals the measure of a person' (Linda Belleville). Look at Paul's reaction to conflict in 1:15—2:4 and/or 2:5–11. How did he cope with it? What might you have said or done? What can we learn?
- There is much about suffering in these chapters (see 1:3–11 and 4:7–18). What insights into suffering can you draw out from either or both of these passages? How far have you had similar experiences?
- Have you been on the giving or receiving end of discipline in church or elsewhere? What did it feel like? How was it handled? What lessons could be learned from 2:5–11?
- Michael B. Thompson writes of 3:18, 'To be a Christian is to change, for God is in the transformation business.' Ponder 3:4—4:6. Try to capture afresh the life-transforming wonder of what God in Christ and through his Spirit has done for you. Which particular aspect or verse most speaks to you? Turn this into an act of praise.
- Most people like to control their circumstances and operate from the position of their strengths. In many ways, Paul's ministry was the precise opposite (see 4:7–18). Might you be most open to God's transforming grace in the very areas that you see as your weakest?

27 February–5 March

1 Death: then what?

2 Corinthians 5:1–10

This is 'a notoriously difficult paragraph', about which the commentators disagree, and yet the subject could hardly be more important. It helps to remember Paul's physical frailty and to read this passage alongside 1 Corinthians 15:35–58 and 2 Corinthians 4:16–18.

Paul uses two pictures to show what happens beyond the grave. First, he pictures our bodies as houses. Our present body is, like a tent, temporary and made from the earth, as was Adam's. It is mortal (v. 4) and corruptible. We may well groan, but we do not want stage two—that is to die and so to be without any dwelling. We long for stage three, our heavenly dwelling. The second picture is that of clothing. Our present clothes are fast wearing out, but on death we do not much want to be unclothed. Rather, we look forward to stage three, to put on eternally new clothes—that is our resurrection bodies—over the top (vv. 1–4).

Paul tells us more about each stage. In stage one, despite our bodies wearing out, we are being inwardly renewed by the Spirit (v. 5; 3:18; 4:16). Stage two is death and beyond, until the judgment (v. 10). Paul would prefer Christ to return during his lifetime and so avoid this 'naked' stage (vv. 3–4), but perhaps, after recent experiences, he is less sure that he will live that long (see 1 Corinthians 15:52: 'we'). Even at this stage, however, the Christian will be 'at home with the Lord' (v. 6; see Philippians 1:23 and Romans 8:38 for the same assurance and wonder). Stage three is the climax, the renewal of creation (Romans 8:22–23) and the receiving of our resurrection bodies, which are made by God in his realm, heaven, and brought to earth for us to wear. The language, like that of 1 Corinthians 15:35–57, hints at some continuity with our present bodies but much more transformation.

Our attitude now should be confidence (v. 6) based on gazing at our future (4:18) and, despite understandable groans (vv. 2, 4), a determination to please Christ whatever happens to us (v. 9). Ultimately we face Christ as judge, though the verdict of acquittal is known already (see also Romans 8:1; 1 Corinthians 3:10–13 on judgment).

What have you learnt about life after death, and how should this affect your life now?

Why is God's renewal of our physical bodies and the cosmos so important?

2 The logic of love

2 Corinthians 5:11—6:2

This is a 'classic' passage. Paul explains himself and the gospel with passion, personal honesty and a wonderful but dense theology that tells us what makes him tick. Most of all, he wants the Corinthians to respond now to God's message of reconciliation and to him as its proclaimer (5:11, 20; 6:1–2).

First, Paul tells them his motives. One is 'fear'—that is, awe and a sense of inadequacy as he thinks of judgment day. It is not fear that he will be condemned (Romans 8:1), though his work could be wasted (1 Corinthians 3:11–15). But above all, his motive is the logic of love (v. 14). As Tom Wright says, 'The logic of love outweighs all other logic known to the human race.' The context strongly suggests that it is Christ's love for Paul rather than Paul's for Christ that compels him. This love focuses on Christ's death, which is Paul's main emphasis here (vv. 14–15, 19, 21), but the resurrection is also mentioned (v. 15). He died for us so that our sins will not be credited to our heavily in-debt account. Instead he reconciles us because, like a sin-offering, he has borne our guilt. This is the ultimate exchange. Christ receives our guilt and punishment, and we receive his status of acquittal and acceptance. All of this is God's doing, through which he creates not just a new people but a whole new world (v. 17).

This affects Paul massively. First, he must now live for Christ (v. 15; see Philippians 1:21). Next, he views people quite differently now, seeing them not primarily as mere human beings but potentially as God's new creations (vv. 16–17). Third, Paul now has a new and supremely wonderful message: reconciliation (v. 19). He is urgent and intense in its proclamation, for he is Christ's ambassador (5:19—6:2).

How far can you truly echo Paul's passion to be a reconciler?
What does God's love in Christ for you make you want to do for him?

3 Open wide your hearts

1/3

2 Corinthians 6:3—7:1

C.K. Barrett refers to these verses as 'an impassioned and almost lyrical passage'. Paul gives 28 marks that distinguish his ministry, because the last thing he wants is that it should be discredited in the Corinthians' eyes. First (vv. 4b–5) he lists ten types of suffering. Paul realized that to do this might be pouring fuel on his opponents' flames of criticism, but these are the very marks that show he follows a crucified Messiah. The most important quality is the first: 'great endurance' (v. 4).

Next come four virtues (v. 6a), two of which, patience and kindness, belong in most of Paul's lists. Verses 6b–7 focus mainly on five of God's provisions for spiritual warfare. A Roman soldier carried a shield for defence on his left arm and a sword and spear in his right hand for attack. Third, Paul lists four ways, each including a positive and negative reaction, in which his ministry is received (vv. 8–9a). Elsewhere he tells us that it is only God's estimate that counts anyway (1 Corinthians 4:3). This is a good antidote to popularity seeking! Paul ends with five frank and paradoxical descriptions of how he often feels (vv. 9b–10).

At the end of this section comes one of Paul's warmest appeals (vv. 11–13). His words and his heart have been open to his spiritual children. Will they not be equally open and vulnerable in return? We need to heed this plea for mutual honesty and vulnerability in today's churches.

Chapter 6:14—7:1 poses several problems. The change of mood and topic is sudden even by Paul's standards, and the vocabulary and style are not typical of Paul either. If you read 6:13 and then 7:2, there can appear to be no break. However, there is no textual evidence that this passage was inserted later, so it is probably wisest to accept it as it stands.

The passage is hard to interpret too! What does 'Do not be yoked together with unbelievers' refer to? It could be about contracting a new marriage (see 1 Corinthians 7:39), but it could refer more widely: 'Don't get involved with non-Christians if their ethical or religious values differ radically from God's.' Paul draws five sharp contrasts and backs them with three Old Testament quotations (v. 16, see Leviticus 26:11–12; v. 17, see Isaiah 52:11; v. 18, see 2 Samuel 7:14). All emphasize that having God as Father is an immense and exclusive privilege. The passage ends with an appeal to holier living based on all this.

Which of Paul's 28 marks do you find most surprising, challenging and important? Try putting the pronoun 'I' instead of Paul's 'we' into verses 3–10. What does true holiness look like? What should you consider avoiding?

4 Sorrow into comfort and joy   2/3

2 Corinthians 7:2–16

Three word-groups dominate this passage: 'sorrow' (perhaps better translated 'regret' or 'grief') comes seven times (vv. 8–10); 'joy' or 'rejoice' comes six times (vv. 4–16); and, supremely, 'comfort' or 'encouragement' has eight occurrences. God himself is the great comforter (see 1:3–4). The opening paragraph (vv. 2–4) is a renewed appeal: 'make room for us in your hearts' (see 6:11, 13). There is a renewed and strong expression of Paul's personal warmth towards the church (v. 4) as well as a denial of an apparent accusation of financial impropriety: 'We have exploited no one,' Paul affirms (v. 2).

Verses 5–7 pick up Paul's dealings with Corinth from way back in 2:2–13. From Ephesus he had journeyed west across Macedonia (northern Greece), hoping to meet Titus and discover the all-important Corinthian reaction to his now lost 'severe' letter (2:2–4). Outer circumstances, perhaps the churches' sufferings in Philippi and Thessalonica, and inner fears, probably about his relationship with Corinth, had made this a hard journey (v. 5); but at last he met Titus, who brought wonderful news. Verses 7b and 11 express, in glowing terms, ten Corinthian reactions to Paul and his letter, and all of them are marvellous.

During Paul's previous visit, an itinerant Christian leader seems to have insulted Paul publicly, demanding from him proof that Christ spoke through him. Worse still, the Corinthians had not stood up and supported him. Paul had left quickly for Ephesus. He wrote the 'severe' letter, chiding the church for their lack of support and demanding that they discipline the man. Amazingly, all of this had happened! (vv. 8–12; 2:5–11).

Paul talks of feeling regret or sorrow when he wrote that letter, but how all of that changed as he heard the results of their 'godly sorrow' (vv. 8–10). It is 'godly' because it led to repentance and so to 'salvation', which is perhaps better translated 'personal wholeness'. Remorse alone is not enough: it is self-destructive and feeds an ever-deepening self-pity, which leads to 'death'. Judas' suicide is a classic example.

Paul's final point is Titus' joy and his own delight that his pride in and boasting to Titus about his Corinthian 'children' has proved true. Titus must have been nervous going to Corinth with such a letter. Now Paul is sending him back to organize the collection (8:6)!

What kinds of actions and words are appropriate to reassure someone of your love for them after a disagreement?

What experience(s) of godly sorrow have you had, and how have they changed you?

5 Finish the job

2 Corinthians 8:1–15

Today we start two chapters on Christian giving, yet the word 'money' never occurs. Relationships are now good enough (7:7–16) for Paul to raise this sensitive subject and he does so with tact, not commanding but advising (vv. 8, 10).

The collection for the poor church in Jerusalem had long been a major concern for Paul (Galatians 2:10; Acts 11:29–30), but this was a special effort, which had started at Corinth a year or more ago (1 Corinthians 16:1–4) and which Titus had rekindled as he delivered the severe letter. They had started well, but got stuck. It is often easier to start than to see through a long and costly project. Paul has received money, and church delegates to bring it, from the churches in Turkey (Acts 20:4). He has also just had a wonderful response from the churches of Macedonia (vv. 1–5). He quotes them as a challenge to the competitive-minded Corinthian church (v. 8), because he hopes that their money will be ready on his arrival.

Paul's motive is his passion for church unity (see Galatians 3:28; Ephesians 2:14–18). He hopes that the Jewish Christians will accept the Gentile Christians as part of the new, expanded people of God. Gentiles, for their part, owe Jews a spiritual debt. (Read Romans 11:13–24, which Paul may have been writing on his present travels.)

'Grace' is Paul's keyword. It comes five times in verses 1–9. It refers not just to God's unmerited love for us, but also to what he does by inspiring in us the 'grace of giving' (v. 7). Supremely, grace refers to Christ (v. 9), God's indescribable gift (9:15). Paul argues that Christ is the litmus test for giving. We need to ponder him when asking 'How much?'

'Equality' (vv. 13–14) is the other criterion, but this does not mean that everyone has the same resources. The rich could not support the poor if this were so (vv. 13–14). It refers to equity of need rather than equality of supply. All should have the basics of food, shelter and clothing. The quotation in verse 15 is from Exodus 16:18, about the manna. The basic needs of all were met. Our giving should be proportionate: ten per cent may be too little for the wealthy and too much for the bereft.

In what spirit should we give? There may be as many as ten clues in verses 1–5. Ask yourself which touches/challenges you most. Ponder also how Western Christians should respond to the principle of equity with the Third World.

6 Being honest and being seen to be honest

2 Corinthians 8:16—9:5

How much of the money raised for good causes actually goes to that cause rather than to those who administer it? We can answer that question now, but how could Paul guarantee honesty in the days before banks, when the gift was lavish (v. 20), and when some at Corinth accused him of corruption (v. 20; 7:2; 12:16–18)?

By the time he wrote 1 Corinthians 16:1–4, Paul had already taken two precautions. The money was to be collected before he came, and the church was to appoint men whom they had approved to take their gift to Jerusalem. Now, perhaps twelve months later and with little collection having been done, Paul takes more pains to avoid criticism in advance (vv. 20–21).

He sends Titus plus two others to Corinth to get the gift ready for when he himself will arrive. Verses 16–24 are his letter recommending them. Titus was keen before Paul asked (v. 17) and this was his second visit. He was one of Paul's closest colleagues. The other two are anonymous 'brothers'. It remains a mystery why Paul does not name them and who they are. Titus, reading out this letter in Corinth, would have presumably named them then. One, '*our* brother' (v. 22), could well have been a Corinthian and a friend of Paul's. '*The* brother' (v. 18) is praised by all the churches and was probably from Macedonia (9:4). He may have been one of the three who took the gifts on after Corinth (see Acts 20:4a).

Paul's fourfold strategy now is laid out in chapter 9. First, he recalls the Corinthians' initial enthusiasm and how it had inspired the Macedonians. Will they live up to it (vv. 1–2)? Next, he urges them to consider their (and Paul's) loss of face should the Macedonians find the collection not ready when they arrive soon with Paul (vv. 3–4). Third, Paul tells them well before he comes, to give them time to get things right (vv. 3, 5). Finally, in the next passage, 9:6–15, Paul promises blessings for generosity.

Encouragingly, we know that this strategy worked. In Romans 15:26–27 Paul writes, 'Macedonia and Achaia [southern Greece] were pleased to make a contribution' and he adds, revealing his motivation, 'and indeed they owe it to them. For if the Gentiles have shared in the Jews' spiritual blessings, they owe it to the Jews to share with them their material blessings.'

What wise financial practices do you find here and what are their current equivalents?

Note the warmth of Paul's remarks about his colleagues and churches. He always sought to show them in their best light. How are you with your Christian colleagues?

Guidelines

You can use these meditations in the same way as last week. As an extra alternative, however, a key phrase is given for each of the five ideas below. This can be used instead of or as well as the idea. If you use a key phrase, try repeating it slowly and often, with pauses, mulling over or basking in it.

* Look in the mirror and then at a photo of yourself from some time ago. How do you feel about ageing? How often do you think about death and beyond? What aspect of Paul's teaching in 5:1–10 do you find helpful? As you meditate, praise God for the future he has for you, and/or share your concerns with him. *Key phrase: 'away from the body and at home with the Lord'* (5:8).
* Paul was thrilled by what God had done for him in Christ. That love was the wellspring of his life and the reason why he was so eager to tell others of God's reconciliation. Read and linger over 5:14–21. Ponder afresh the wonder of the cross. Picture yourself as an ambassador with a vital message from your king. With whom should it be shared? *Key phrase: 'Christ's love compels us'* (5:14).
* How easy do you find it to 'open wide your heart'? Could or should you be more open with any particular person, especially any church leader? *Key phrase: 'as servants of God we commend ourselves in every way'* (6:3).
* Chapter 7 is full of the joy of reconciliation. Thank God for situations in your life, in your church or in the world where there has been reconciliation. *Key phrase: 'godly sorrow brings repentance that leads to salvation'* (7:10).
* Ponder any of these three key phrases from chapter 8, and apply them in praise or prayer: *'Now finish the work'* (8:11); *'Excel in this grace of giving'* (8:7); *'Though he was rich, yet for your sakes he became poor, so that you through his poverty might become rich'* (8:9).

1 God's economy or ours?

2 Corinthians 9:6–15

Paul's deep theology lies behind even his most practical teaching, and never more so than in these chapters on giving money. God is the great giver, as is proved supremely by his gift of Christ (v. 15). God receives praise and thanks in response (v. 12; see 1:11; 4:15). This is God's 'economy' for himself and for his church. Money was a topic often on Jesus' lips too. Why do we so often shun it as Christians?

Verses 6–7 lay out three principles. First, the more you give, the more you receive back (v. 6), but only in order that you may give away even more (vv. 8b, 11). Second, each person individually should think through the amount he or she gives. There should be no undue outside pressure. Third, there should be no reluctance, but rather 'hilarity'—the literal meaning of 'cheerful'. Most of us will have experienced the joy of spending generously on a loved one. As Jesus said, truly 'it is more blessed to give than to receive' (Acts 20:35). Such is God's economy.

The rest of the passage can be misread as suggesting that the generous giver gains financially. Certainly verse 8, with its four occurrences of 'all' and the phrase 'you will abound', stresses God as our great giver. Verse 9, quoting Psalm 112:9, refers not to God but to the person who gives. The impact of their righteous gift goes on and on. But the point of this is to enable yet more giving. The harvest of our gifts is enlarged, as is our store of seed for next year's giving, so that we can be generous on 'every occasion' (vv. 10–11).

Everybody wins. Givers can give even more. Recipients benefit and grow closer to and pray more for the givers (a major blessing for both the Jerusalem Jewish Christians and the Gentile ones in Corinth and elsewhere). Recipients will thank and praise God even more (vv. 11–13). Supremely, God receives ever more of the praise due for his surpassing grace; and so the virtuous spiral of self-giving love climbs ever upwards. How can Paul or we find words for the climax of all this, which is the gift of Christ (vv. 14–15)? Paul bursts into praise and so should we. And the collection does seem to have been made (Romans 15:26).

What can you do to foster extravagant grace in your church?
What is stopping your own giving from being more cheerful or hilarious?

2 Paul in defence and on the attack

2 Corinthians 10:1–18

What a sudden change of mood—from warmth to a strident and impassioned defence! Are chapters 10—13 part of another letter, perhaps the 'severe' one? Many think so, but there is no textual evidence. It could be that Paul had just received bad news of renewed opposition and support for the new teachers who had attacked him so strongly before. In verses 1–11 he replies to the critics and in verses 12–18 he attacks them.

'He is all fine talk at a distance but subservient face to face' (v. 1). 'He only uses ordinary arguments. You never see dramatic acts of spiritual power from him as you do from us' (v. 2). Paul replies that his 'meekness and gentleness' (meaning 'strength under control') aim to imitate Christ. He does not want to be 'bold' or 'frighten' them, but he will if they force him into it by remaining disloyal when he arrives (vv. 2, 6, 9–11). He will use God's weapon of truth. Wrong thinking underlies much of their opposition.

Paul's critics claimed to have, from Christ, a greater authority than Paul. Perhaps one of them had known Jesus personally. Paul quotes his own experience of the risen Christ (v. 7); but he has used his authority to build up the Corinthian church. The opponents are pulling it down (v. 8).

Paul could not win. The critics accused his letters of terrifying the church and then said that his words were unimpressive and his physical appearance off-putting. Paul may have agreed (1 Corinthians 2:3–5; 2 Corinthians 12:7–10). We have a description of Paul written 100 years later: 'a man small of stature, with a bald head and crooked legs, in a good state of body, with eyebrows meeting and nose somewhat hooked, full of friendliness.' Early church mosaics agree, and are unflattering!

But Paul refuses to play their game of comparisons and commendations (vv. 12, 17–18). His authority comes from the 'field' and 'proper limits' that God assigned him (vv. 13–16). Paul is referring to the Galatians 2:1–10 agreement with the Jerusalem leaders: Paul would go to the Gentiles and Peter to the Jews. Paul also limited himself to pioneer areas (Romans 15:20). Corinth met all these criteria. They were *his* 'field', not the intruders'. Paul prayed that the church would reach its neighbourhood (and perhaps it had: see 1:1); and that it would be his base for 'regions beyond' (v. 16, perhaps a reference to other Balkan countries or Greek islands). This disunity was stopping evangelism. It often does.

How can we fight spiritual battles in Christ's meek and gentle spirit?

In what ways do we make comparisons between Christian leaders?

3 Super-apostles or false apostles?

2 Corinthians 11:1–21a

Paul describes what he is about to write as 'a little of my foolishness', although the 'foolishness' only really begins in 11:22. He is embarrassed about it (vv. 1, 17), and speaks with irony (v. 1), sarcasm (vv. 19–21) and bitter criticism (vv. 13–15) of those who have forced him into it (12:11). C.K. Barrett comments, 'Being a fool for Christ sometimes meant answering a fool according to his folly.'

Verses 2–5 give three reasons for the Corinthians to 'put up' with this foolishness. First, Paul's motive is the'godly jealousy'of the bride-to-be's father as he ensures her virginity while awaiting the wedding (that is, Christ's return). Second, Paul fears that the intruders may have started to seduce some Corinthians, as the serpent did Eve. They are putting up with the 'other' Jesus, different Spirit and different gospel far too easily. Third, Paul is not inferior to these 'super' but false (v. 13) apostles.

They criticize Paul as an untrained speaker (10:10), and he admits this (v. 6; see 1 Corinthians 2:1). But he does have knowledge—that is, of the gospel. They also accuse him of lack of love (v. 11) in not accepting 'pay' while with the Corinthians. Acts 18:3–5 shows that he plied his trade in Corinth till Timothy arrived from Macedonia with money for him from those churches. It was his policy to preach the gospel free of charge in a new city (v. 7) and to be supported by them later, when he moved on. In 1 Corinthians 9:18; he says that Christian workers have the right to be paid but, for Paul, his practice exemplifies Christ's principle of making others rich through his poverty (8:9; compare 11:7). Paul is thus distinct from the super-apostles, and he intends to remain so. 'Humility and self-sacrifice are often misunderstood by those who do not themselves frequently practise it' (C.K. Barrett).

The bitter attack in verses 13–15 and 20 reminds us of the prophets and Jesus' own condemnation of those who lead astray his 'little ones' (Matt.18:6–7). The super-apostles' emphasis on the spectacular and on their qualifications and their self-opinionated assertiveness contrast with Paul's suffering and Jesus' way of the cross.

What steps can a church take to prevent the abuse of power by its leaders?
How should you deal with criticism that attacks the motives of your best-intended actions?

4 Power made perfect in weakness

2 Corinthians 11:21b—12:10

Roman society expected its citizens to boast of their achievements. The 'intruder' teachers at Corinth clearly boasted (11:21) and forced a reluctant Paul to do so; but he reverses their criteria as he starts (11:22), continues (12:1) and completes (12:11) his 'boast'. Even so, he is uncomfortable (11:17, 21, 23; 12:1, 11). He would rather they judged him on their experience of him with them. Nevertheless, what he says now will be God's truth, no exaggeration (11:30–31). Indeed, he could say more but he won't (12:6).

Paul's list (vv. 21b–33) highlights the very experiences that most people would be too ashamed to mention. It shows how even the book of Acts only mentions a small proportion of his sufferings, and takes no account of the eleven years (AD56–67) still remaining before his execution! First, his Jewish pedigree (v. 22) is equal to the critics'. Next, his service record is far superior (vv. 23–25). Surely his courage and stamina must have won many for Christ! He lists eight travel dangers, many deprivations (v. 27) and the pressure of and care for the churches he had founded (vv. 28–29). The climax is his escape from Damascus (vv. 32–33; see Acts 9:23–25) about three years after his conversion (Galatians 1:17–18). Rome's highest military honour, the *Corona Muralis*, was awarded to the foolhardy soldier first over the wall into a besieged town under attack. Paul instead escapes humiliatingly in a basket. Boasting is reversed!

The 'intruders' boasted of their ecstatic experiences, so Paul does the same (12:1–6), but with a decisive difference (12:7–10). Acts tells us of several visions (16:9; 18:9; 22:17–21; 23:11; 27:23), but Paul mentions only one, 14 years earlier—around AD42. Uniquely he speaks of himself in the third person ('I know a man…'). This may be due to his especial dislike of this kind of boasting. He is reticent too about his state during the vision and what he heard in it (12:2–4). The 'third heaven' or 'paradise' are two Jewish descriptions of the immediate presence of God and his angels. It was then that Paul was first aware of the 'thorn in his flesh'. This may have been a physical ailment, perhaps concerning his eyesight (Galatians 4:14–15). Instead of removing it at Paul's triple request, as the 'intruders' no doubt expected Paul to claim, God said 'No', both to keep Paul from pride and especially to display the vastness of his power seen in Paul's human weakness (12:9–10). Paul, however, is delighted (12:10). Verse 9 is the theme of this whole letter.

How important for Christian leadership are ecstatic experiences and suffering?

What is your 'thorn'? What has God said to you about it? How have you reacted in the past and how do you react now?

5 Preparing for Paul's third visit

2 Corinthians 12:11—13:4

At last Paul has finished 'boasting' and making a fool of himself (12:11). He has shown that he is not inferior to the intruder 'super-apostles', even by their misguided criteria. With irony he accepts being God's 'nobody'. But the Corinthians should have spoken up for Paul and his gospel message against the intruders. Then he need not have undertaken this 'boasting' at all. He too has the marks of an apostle: 'signs, wonders and miracles' (12:12; see Mark 16:17, 20; Acts 2:22; also Paul's miracles in Acts). They themselves were his chief 'sign' performed in Corinth 'with great perseverance'.

Paul is about to make his third visit and again he will finance his own needs, despite the protests of some (12:13–15) and the accusations of trickery by others (12:16), presumably implying that he would help himself to the money collected for Jerusalem. Paul uses irony ('forgive me this wrong', 12:13), and evidence (their experience of Titus' recent visit (12:18; see 7:13–16; 8:6), to parry these painful innuendoes. His reasons remain the principle of God's grace rather than a consumer mentality, and the fact that he is their spiritual father and so should provide for them, not vice versa (12:14). One of Paul's tenderest expressions of love then leads to an appeal to them to respond in love to him (12:15).

Paul has fears for his coming visit (12:20—13:4). Both he and the church may be disappointed by each other's behaviour then. Paul fears that he may find huge dissension (12:20) caused by the intruders. Note the chaos caused by sins of the tongue. He also fears that he will see gross sexual sins still being practised, despite supposed repentance (12:21; 13:2). There are echoes of both these offences in 1 Corinthians 1 and 5. Paul's three visits and warnings (13:1) comprise the three witnesses required in law by Deuteronomy 19:15 (see also Matthew 18:16). The Corinthians may be disappointed in Paul's 'power' too, as he does not 'spare' the impenitent (13:2). The punishment would probably be exclusion from Christian fellowship and communion (1 Corinthians 5:1–13). Paul realizes that he may be humiliated again in front of them (12:21), perhaps by the intruders' public questioning of whether Christ spoke through Paul at all (13:3). But this would be God's doing ('my God will humble me', 12:21). Just as Christ's death and resurrection showed God's strange mixture of strength and weakness, so God's apostle, Paul, will be at God's strongest in his weakness (13:3–4; 12:9–10).

What is the role today of signs and wonders in planting a new church or renewing an established one?

Which of the problems mentioned in this passage do you struggle with most in your personal life?

6 Who will pass the test?

2 Corinthians 13:5–13

The Corinthians have put Paul to the test. Now they should test themselves (v. 5). Fun quizzes tell us how good a husband or wife we are, but what about testing ourselves on our Christian lives—a spiritual check-up? Paul uses several phrases for being a Christian: 'in the faith'; 'Christ in you'; 'acting for the truth' (vv. 5, 8). Is the risen and crucified life of Christ evident in you? When you listen to what you say, do you sound like Jesus speaking? Do you ask yourself, 'What would Jesus do or say?'

If they are Christians and pass the test, then so does Paul, their spiritual father (v. 6). But Paul's great concern is about their deeds as evidence of their faith. He prays that they never, ever do evil. Indeed, their acts should be lovely to behold ('right', vv. 7–8). Their well-being ('strength', v. 9) is more important than his appearing 'weak'. Being strong means being firm in the faith (v. 5) and 'of one mind' (v. 11).

Verses 10–13 are Paul's final thoughts. First he repeats his reasons for writing so firmly. He wants to avoid being firm on arrival in Corinth. His aim is to build them up, not tear them down (v. 10). This is a key phrase (see 10:8; 12:19; note Paul's own call in Galatians 1:15, echoing Jeremiah's call in Jeremiah 1:5). Next come five brief exhortations (often translated in different ways): 'cheer up, set matters right (this Greek word is used for mending nets in Mark 1:19; see also v. 9), exhort one another, be of one mind and live at peace'. Then 'the God of love and peace will be with you' (v. 11). The kiss of peace, most often on the hand, cheek or forehead, was the traditional greeting (Luke 7:45; Romans 16:16). Paul's fellow Christians in Macedonia, where he was while writing this letter, sent greetings (v. 13).

Paul ends with 'the grace'—an extended, memorable and marvellous blessing. The phrase 'the love of God' comes only here in the New Testament, but a God who loves and is to be loved was a novel idea in that world and ours. The 'fellowship of the Spirit' probably refers to the oneness that the believers should experience with one another. All three persons of the Godhead are placed side by side here, anticipating a later century's doctrine of the Trinity.

By what signs can a person know whether he or she is a Christian?

Which of Paul's final words is most relevant to you at this moment?

Guidelines

This section follows the same pattern as the previous 'Guidelines'.

- The Christian giving of money is a major theme in this letter and in Christ's teaching. Re-read 9:6–15 and ponder the spirit in which to give (9:6–7) and the results of giving (9:8–14). Then picture the crib and the cross and focus your thoughts on the supreme giver (9:15). *Key phrase: 'Thanks be to God for his indescribable gift!'*

- Justifying one's actions and motives, as Paul does in 10:1—11:33, is embarrassing, and it is all too easy for it to turn into an unpleasant counter-attack (11:4–15). In what circumstances might you, like Paul, be forced into this position? Paul rejected contemporary criteria for respectability and 'boasted' instead of his sufferings and weaknesses (11:22—12:10). Is a comparable pathway open to you? Ponder Paul's motives. *Key phrases: 'I am jealous for you with a godly jealousy' (11:2) and 'everything we do, dear friends, is for your strengthening' (12:19).*

- It is hard to see debilitating disease—a 'thorn in the flesh'—as other than a satanic messenger (12:7). Think of personal experiences similar to this. Read again Paul's reaction and God's reply (12:8–9). Ask God to enable you to say and mean 12:10. *Key phrase: 'My grace is sufficient for you, for my power is made perfect in weakness' (12:9).*

- Chapter 13:14 can lay claim to being Paul's finest last verse. Ponder each person of the Trinity and the role God plays in your life and your church's. Say 'the grace' afresh as you think of ever new examples of Christ's grace, God's love and the shared oneness given by the Spirit. *Key phrase: 'May the grace of the Lord Jesus Christ, and the love of God, and the fellowship of the Holy Spirit be with you all' (13:14).*

FURTHER READING

Michael B. Thompson, *Transforming Grace*, BRF, 1998. A study of 2 Corinthians, with six weeks' worth of notes and questions applying to Christian leaders.

Tom Wright, *Paul for Everyone: 2 Corinthians*, SPCK, 2003. Gives Wright's own translation and takes a fresh look at the text over 36 readings.

C.K. Barrett, *Second Epistle to the Corinthians*, A & C Black, 1972. Classic commentary on Barrett's own English text. Deeper and less applied.

Linda Belleville, *2 Corinthians*, IVP, 1996? Over 350 pages: quite detailed, conservative. Some application to life now.

JOSHUA

The story of Joshua is to be found predominantly in the book that bears his name, but he is also mentioned in the books of Exodus, Numbers, Deuteronomy and Judges. He appears as one of the leaders of the Israelites during the years of wandering in the wilderness, and ultimately as the one who will succeed Moses in leading the chosen people into the promised land.

The context and significance of the figure of Joshua is to some extent paralleled in the canonical context and significance of the book of Joshua. Although it stands outside the Pentateuch, there is a sense in which it represents the culmination of the promises made to the ancestors of Israel, particularly Abraham, that God's people will have a future and a land in which to dwell. But it also stands at the beginning of that great sweeping account of God's people from their settlement in the promised land to their loss first of the northern kingdom of Israel to the Assyrians and then of the southern kingdom of Judah to the Babylonians. This account (comprising the books of Joshua, Judges, Samuel and Kings) is sometimes known as the Deuteronomistic History, because it may have been shaped by those who were responsible for the book of Deuteronomy and who shared the outlook of that book. Their concern is not just to give an account of past events but to try to understand what led to the loss of the land given to their ancestors. As we shall see, the answer has something to do with reward for obedience to the will of God and punishment for disobedience. What purport to be the words of Joshua to his generation are the words of the Deuteronomists to their own generation, reminding them that when their ancestors were obedient they were rewarded with land. The God who had punished this later generation with the loss of land could restore them if only they would be obedient.

The comments that follow are based on the New Revised Standard Version.

1 Ready for action

Deuteronomy 31:1–14, 23

The work of Moses, the servant of God, is coming to an end. His task is to lead the Israelites to the very borders of the promised land, but he is not to be allowed to enter the land himself. The privilege of actually leading his people into the land is to fall to Joshua. Joshua has already been mentioned in the biblical narratives. In the book of Exodus he is involved in a defeat of the Amalekites (Exodus 17:8–13) and he is mentioned as a right-hand man of Moses (Exodus 24:13; 33:11). In the book of Numbers he is mentioned as one of those sent to spy out the land of Canaan, his name being changed from Hoshea to Joshua (Numbers 13:16), and as one of only two of the wilderness generation (along with Caleb) who will be allowed to enter the land (Numbers 14:30, 38; 26:65; 32:12). He is to be Moses' successor (Numbers 27:18–22) and, along with the priest Eleazar, he is to be involved in the apportioning of the land to the tribes (Numbers 34:17).

Several of these themes are picked up in these verses near the end of the book of Deuteronomy, which describe Joshua's commissioning. His activity is immediately placed in the context of God's activity (v. 3) and, significantly, it is closely related to the making of a copy of the law and instructions for its regular reading (vv. 9–13). In a favourite phrase in this part of the narrative, Joshua is encouraged to 'be strong and bold' (vv. 6, 7; see also Joshua 1:6, 7, 9, 18, where the NRSV translates it 'be strong and [very] courageous'). The reason that he can demonstrate these qualities is precisely because God will be with him (see v. 8). Later it is mentioned that, as a result of his commissioning, Joshua was 'full of the spirit of wisdom' (Deuteronomy 34:9). His years of apprenticeship to Moses, the various types of experience gained, the divine commission and the assurance of God's presence have made Joshua ready for action.

2 The work must go on

As we move into the book of Joshua, there are obvious continuities with what has gone before in Deuteronomy, and it is clear that we are still reading from the same work, despite the present book divisions. Moses is now dead, but his work (more correctly, God's work) must continue, now under the leadership of Joshua. Just as God has been with Moses, so he will be with Joshua (v. 5).

The geographical setting changes, in that the story of Moses ends outside the land, and now the scene shifts to the imminent crossing of the Jordan and the taking of the land. Verse 4 presents a highly idealistic view of the land; what is indicated here is a great tract of land, much greater than was ever occupied by the Israelites. Verse 5 is also idealistic in suggesting that the whole operation would be carried out with no one able to withstand Joshua. Indeed, one view of the book of Joshua is that it primarily preserves a story of a trouble-free possession of the land, thanks to God's presence and involvement, of the type that might have been used later in celebrating God's deeds in worship. This may be true of much of the book, but it has also been suggested that the Deuteronomistic History has undergone a careful revision: in the book of Joshua, this is seen in several additions, which modify the view that all the land was conquered in one great military sweep and stress that success was conditional upon obedience on the law. Perhaps such a revision appears in verses 7–9a, where the emphasis shifts from a tone of encouragement to an injunction to obedience to the law and to the importance of meditating upon it continually.

The final form of the text, as it has come down to us, presents us with a call not just to theological reflection upon God's word but to action as God's co-workers. The assurance to Joshua that God is with him (v. 9b) is followed by an instruction to the officers of the people to urge the people to prepare for action. The work must go on.

3 Remember what God has done

There are a number of passages in the book of Joshua which can be described as etiologies, in that they purport to explain the origin of some natural feature or phenomenon, or some structure, custom or practice that was current at the time the traditions were written or related. A particular type of etiology seeks to explain why people or places were given their particular names. There has been a tendency to assume that such traditions can have little or no historical value, and this is doubtless true of many of them, but it must be remembered that etiological elements may sometimes have become attached to older traditions.

This episode in Joshua 4 probably seeks in part to explain the presence of a feature of the sanctuary at Gilgal (some standing stones) and perhaps also the name of Gilgal itself (which may mean 'circle', the allusion perhaps being to a stone circle). The uncertainty over precisely where the stones were set up—either 'where they camped' (v. 8) or 'in the middle of the Jordan' (v. 9)—could be a clue to the fact that different sources may underlie the tradition as we now have it. But the setting up of these stones as a 'memorial for ever' (v. 7) also acts as a way of reminding the people what God has done for them in enabling them to enter the land. The exodus from Egypt had involved a remarkable crossing of a stretch of water, seen as a sign of God's involvement. Now the entry into the land is accompanied by a similar guarantee of God's presence with the people. (Here, as elsewhere, the ark of the covenant serves as a symbol of God's presence; it is noteworthy that the ark often features in military contexts.) The stones are to remind people for ever of what God has done.

4 It's hard to believe

Joshua 6:12–21

Here we read part of the most familiar of the stories of the conquest: how the walls of Jericho came tumbling down. It is presented as a miraculous defeat of a strongly fortified city and, as such, for many it is hard to believe that such a thing could have taken place. Attempts have been made to offer rationalistic explanations for what happened. Perhaps it was an earthquake that brought the walls tumbling down, or perhaps the combined effect of the tramping of countless feet, accompanied by shouting and trumpet blasts, could have brought about a weakening of the walls and hence their collapse. Those who look to archaeology for confirmation are disappointed to learn that there is little evidence that Jericho was a fortified city at the time usually suggested for these events, but such explanations tend to miss the point. The story is telling later generations that if God's servants will be obedient, remarkable things can happen.

There are other features of this story which are hard to believe. Today's readers will be perplexed by the thought that it might be God's will that a whole city, with almost all its inhabitants, should be destroyed, and explanations along the lines that this is a sign of God's power or God's judgment only partially solve the problem.

It may also be hard to believe that a prostitute, Rahab, and her family should be the only ones spared (v. 17). A clue to the answer is perhaps to be found in Joshua 2:12, where the Hebrew word underlying what the NRSV translates as 'deal kindly' is better translated as 'steadfast love', 'constant love' or 'covenant loyalty'. It refers to God's attitude to those who have entered into a covenant with him, and to the attitude they are expected to show to God and to one another. Here is a message about the rewards of loyalty and obedience. It is noteworthy that, in the great chapter on faith, the writer of Hebrews makes no mention of our hero, Joshua, but does mention Rahab, whose faith was shown in what she did for the spies (Hebrews 11:30–31). God sometimes uses the most surprising and unlikely people in achieving his purposes. Here is encouragement, even if at times it is hard to believe.

5 Obedience is essential

Joshua 7:1–15

Underlying this passage is another concept that creates immense difficulties for today's reader. This is the notion that a whole city, for example, might be devoted to God, but as a form of sacrifice in which all people and living creatures would be destroyed and all the property handed over to God, rather than becoming plunder for the conquerors. So the passage opens with the statement that Achan failed to observe this act of devotion and took some of the spoils for himself (see 7:20–21).

There is dramatic irony in the way the story is told. The reader knows of Achan's disobedience but, according to the story, Joshua does not, so he is at a loss to understand why the capture of the city of Ai (which should have been straightforward) has gone horribly and inexplicably wrong. Joshua's reaction is to blame God, an all-too-human response even from a great hero. Joshua has to be told that the fault lies elsewhere and that God cannot be blamed for what has been caused by human sin, and the passage stresses that the act of disobedience has to be put right before the people can hope to prosper once more. (There is also an etiological element that becomes clear only at the end of the chapter, in verses 24–26: the name of Achan recalls the name of the Valley of Achor and the word meaning 'trouble'.)

The passage also reflects one of the tensions revealed in various places in the Hebrew Bible—between individual and collective responsibility. The chapter begins with a statement that 'the Israelites broke faith' (v. 1), but it soon becomes clear that it is one individual who has done so. Somehow, the sin of an individual is thought to affect everyone, and so people can hide behind the possibility that they are being punished for someone else's sin. The great prophets Jeremiah and Ezekiel, reflecting on the proverb 'The parents have eaten sour grapes, and the children's teeth are set on edge' (Jeremiah 31:29, Ezekiel 18:2), stress that individuals are responsible for their own sin and so for their own obedience.

6 What's in a name?
Joshua 8:10–19, 28

Once matters had been put right after the disobedience of Achan, the next stage of the occupation could take place. The great city of Ai was captured as the result of a cunning stratagem to lure the inhabitants out of the city and ambush them. At first sight, this might seem much more plausible than the remarkable destruction of Jericho, but again the results of archaeological excavation challenge us to look a little deeper, since it seems that Ai (assuming the site has been correctly identified) was not occupied at the time usually suggested for the so-called conquest, towards the end of the second millennium BC. It has been suggested that the sites of Bethel and Ai, only about a mile apart, may have become confused. Their proximity is noted in our passage (v. 12), and there is some evidence that Bethel underwent a rather turbulent history at that time.

There is a more intriguing possibility, however. The name Ai means 'ruin', prompting us to ask why a city would be called 'ruin'. Interestingly, the modern name of the likely site is et-Tell; the word *tell* prefixes the names of many ancient sites and signifies a mound which has been built up as the result of a succession of occupations. So the modern name mirrors the ancient name. Perhaps the Israelites called this city 'ruin' precisely because that is what it was when they first occupied it—but the name provided an opportunity to tell a story that contributed to the presentation of the heroic achievements of the great commander Joshua and, more importantly, to the glory of the God who inspired him.

Guidelines

Joshua often appears not just as Moses' assistant and successor but almost as a second Moses. Both lead the people across a stretch of water (see Exodus 14:21–25; Joshua 3:7–17), both are required to remove their sandals because they are standing on holy ground (see Exodus 3:5; Joshua 5:15), and both inscribe the law on stones (see Exodus 34:27–28; Joshua 8:32; 24:26). Particularly noteworthy is that both are described as the 'servant of the Lord' (see, for example, Joshua 1:1; 24:29). In indicating these parallels, perhaps those who edited these traditions are stressing that, for God's work to go on, a succession of obedient servants is required, and the story of Joshua invites us to give thanks for that succession of individuals through whom God has guided his people down the ages.

The image of 'crossing the Jordan' as a way of referring to entering fully into God's presence is a familiar one, for example in the words of hymn writers ('When I tread the verge of Jordan... land me safe on Canaan's side', William Williams; 'Bring me safe through Jordan to thy home above', Edmond Budry). They may have in mind God's heavenly abode, but for Joshua the call was to a life of down-to-earth obedience.

1 Keeping your word?

Joshua 9:16–27

One of the widely held attitudes in the ancient Near East, and certainly in ancient Israel, seems to have been a sense of responsibility for those members of society who were less able to fend for themselves or protect themselves. This was a particular concern of the king (see, for example, Psalm 72:1–4, 12–14), but it was expected of the populace as a whole (see, for example, Exodus 22:21–22; Deuteronomy 10:17–19). Among those in special need of care were members of their own society such as widows, orphans and the underprivileged, but those who were aliens (or sojourners) resident in the land were also afforded protection.

The background to this passage is that the Gibeonites, having heard what Joshua has done to Jericho and Ai, are afraid that they will suffer the same fate. They have therefore hit on a plan to make it appear that they have come from a far country (9:6), having heard what God has done for the Israelites, and that they wish to enter into a treaty. So Joshua has made peace with them and guaranteed their safety with a treaty (9:15). As our passage opens, the stratagem has been realized, and perhaps the natural instinct would be to pay back the Gibeonites for their deception. But a treaty has been made, and an undertaking to protect their lives has been given. The leaders of the people fear God's wrath if they go back on their word; nor is Joshua willing to break the treaty, even when the Gibeonites confess their deception. They do not escape entirely, however: they are allotted a menial status as 'hewers of wood and drawers of water' for the house of God (v. 23). This passage too has something to say about obedience. The Gibeonites entered into a treaty falsely and so became slaves. Joshua and the leaders of the Israelites set a finer example, even in a situation where they could be forgiven for not doing so, by keeping their word.

2 With God on our side...

The book of Joshua describes how, in the aftermath of the destruction of Jericho and Ai and the treaty with the Gibeonites, a coalition of five kings came together to besiege Gibeon. Here again we meet several of those difficult elements of which there are a number in the book of Joshua, and with which today's readers may be uncomfortable. One of these is the concept of 'holy war', by no means limited to this book but occurring prominently within it. Some prefer to refer to use the designation 'wars of Yahweh', a term which perhaps reduces the suggestion that such wars were holy. Indeed, Numbers 21:14 suggests that there may have existed a 'Book of the Wars of Yahweh'. The distinguishing feature of such wars was that God was presented as an active participant (see v. 14). A number of the elements that recur regularly in the various accounts can be seen here:

- the 'handing-over formula' (v. 8: 'I have handed them over to you').
- a stress on God's participation, often in a superhuman or miraculous way, here in the throwing down of huge hailstones and in the sun standing still (vv. 11, 13).
- the reduction of the enemy to a state of panic or confusion (v. 10).
- an emphasis on complete destruction (v. 11b: 'there were more who died because of the hailstones than the Israelites killed with the sword').

It is another ancient source, the 'Book of Jashar', which is quoted in this passage, raising the possibility that our writers did have access to ancient written traditions. It may be that the story of a victory at Gibeon has been produced to explain a well-known snippet of poetry and inserted at an appropriate point in the account of the conquest. Such traditions underline the point that, in situations where human strength is inadequate, God stands alongside those who are loyal to him.

3 Promises fulfilled...?

The feature of a storm as the means whereby God brought about a victory, seen in the previous passage, recalls the story of how Deborah and Barak were enabled to defeat Sisera thanks to a thunderstorm causing the enemy chariots to become bogged down (Judges 4—5). The writer of Judges 4 seems to have been in some confusion, associating that victory with the reign of Jabin, king of Hazor, and making Sisera the commander of Jabin's armies (Judges 4:2). According to the book of Joshua, the defeat of Jabin and the capture of Hazor were the crowning glory of Joshua's achievements, even though they are not described in such detail as the defeats of Jericho and Ai. That this was considered no mean achievement is suggested in the comment, 'Before that time Hazor was the head of all those kingdoms' (v. 10b). Archaeology has confirmed that Hazor was a huge city in its heyday.

The description of the defeat of Hazor leads into a summary of Joshua's achievements. He has conquered all the land and defeated its kings (vv. 16–18). He has even wiped out those legendary giants, the Anakim ('the long-necked ones'): traditions seem to have persisted that there were previous inhabitants of the land who were of exceptional stature (see, for example, Deuteronomy 1:28; 2:20–21; 3:11). So now Joshua has completed the task started by Moses, and 'the land had rest from war' (v. 23). The next chapter stresses the joint nature of this venture, giving a comprehensive list of the kings defeated by Moses (12:1–6) and those defeated by Joshua (12:7–24). Our passage stresses that Joshua was following instructions that God had given to Moses (vv. 15, 20, 23), but he was thereby also setting the seal on the promises made by God to Israel's ancestors, that they would have a land in which to dwell. The promises are at last fulfilled.

4 ... or are they?

Joshua 13:1–7

Treatments of the book of Joshua often divide the book into two main sections: chapters 1—12, which describe the conquest of the land; and chapters 13—21, which describe the division of the land, chapters 22—24 forming a sort of postscript. Chapters 13—21 present a challenge to people who set out to read the Bible from cover to cover and who have made it thus far, not having been put off by lists of clean and unclean animals in Leviticus, for example. Here are more lists—lists of cities and lists of boundaries—and much ink has been spilt in the attempt to demonstrate the possible origins of these lists. But they are not simply to be dismissed as dull and uninteresting. They demonstrate that God has fulfilled his promises, a point which is made clear at the very end of the section (21:43–45), and they have been described as the heart of the book of Joshua. The chapters hint at the complexity that was the people of Israel, and perhaps also at the magnitude of the task of giving any sort of unity to such disparate groups.

Right at the outset, there is mention of the fact that all is not quite as straightforward as it has been made to seem. In verses 1–7 there are brief details of land that has not yet been conquered, although there is the assurance that God himself will drive out those who remain of the previous inhabitants, and that therefore the allocation to the tribes can go ahead. This is one of a number of passages in the book of Joshua (see also, for example, 15:63; 16:10; 17:12–13) which imply a picture, akin to that of Judges 1, of a rather less complete conquest and a more fragmented occupation. It is noteworthy that the editorial process has resulted in the events described in Judges 1 being placed 'after the death of Joshua' (Judges 1:1), even though that is not in fact the case (see Judges 2:6–8). Perhaps this was an act of deference to the 'conquering hero' picture which is the predominant view of the book of Joshua.

5 Telling God's story

Joshua 24:1–15

One of the enigmas of the book of Joshua is the presence, at the end, of two valedictory speeches by Joshua. The first of these (Joshua 23) is not located geographically, is said to have happened 'a long time afterwards' (23:1), and is addressed to all Israel as well as to the leaders of the people (23:2). It contains an exhortation to obey the law of Moses (23:6) and a reminder that God has fulfilled his promises (23:14), two of the recurring themes of the book.

The second speech, in chapter 24, is the one on which we shall concentrate here. It is addressed to a gathering of the tribal leaders and is set in Shechem—perhaps surprisingly, since Shechem falls outside

Joshua's main sphere of activity. One suggestion to account for the presence of the two addresses is that some Shechemite traditions have been added to an earlier version of Joshua's activity. There has been much debate over the origins of this chapter, and whether it is relatively early or late. Some have argued that it reflects a genuine tradition of a gathering of tribal leaders, perhaps when tribes who had not been principally involved in the events of the exodus and conquest were called upon to accept Yahweh, the God who had led the people during those episodes. Another suggestion is that the chapter reflects the form of a religious ceremony in which representatives of the tribes would renew their commitment to the covenant, perhaps annually. What *is* clear is that Joshua calls upon the people to make a choice (v. 15), and the basis on which they are to make the choice is God's own account, spoken through Joshua, of what God has already done for them.

A noteworthy feature of the speech is its alternation between third and second person. See, for example, verse 6a: 'When I brought *your ancestors* out of Egypt, *you* came to the sea'. What God has done for the ancestors, he has, in a real sense, done for the present generation. So a choice must be made, and Joshua declares that he and his family have made their choice. Others must now choose, based on the evidence of God's story.

6 Challenge and commitment

Joshua 24:16–28

In the Pentateuch, the promises to the ancestors of Israel are based firmly on what God will do for them. In the previous passage, Joshua has reminded the people that God has kept his word, so they must make a decision for or against God. The challenge has been put and now the people make their choice: 'Far be it from us that we should forsake the Lord' (v. 16). But Joshua's reaction is surprising! 'You cannot serve the Lord…' he tells them (v. 19). The people seem to have been convinced and to have responded as Joshua had hoped, but he still finds it necessary to challenge them further. Are they really convinced? Will they really accept the challenge? When they insist that they mean what they say, Joshua ensures that they cannot forget their promises by writing down the terms of the agreement, and setting up a stone to act as a witness (vv. 25–26).

The presence of this passage may reflect the fact that these words, which purport to be those of Joshua to his own generation, are ultimately addressed to a later generation who have lost their land, by those trying to find an explanation that makes sense in terms of their faith. They had gained the land when they had been obedient; therefore, it must have been disobedience that lost them the land. Time and again the people of Israel professed their commitment to God, but time and again they were disobedient to God's will, particularly in forsaking their own God for other gods. So the focus of the chapter is on choosing Yahweh rather than the gods of the Mesopotamians, Egyptians or Canaanites. Words are easy, but promises to God are not to be undertaken lightly. In challenging the people of his time, and calling for a firm commitment, Joshua speaks to people of faith of all generations.

Guidelines

Joshua is presented as a second Moses, as we have seen, and provides an example of obedient earthly leadership of God's people. Parallels have also been noted between Joshua and another important Old Testament figure, King Josiah. Both proclaimed the law of Moses to the people and led the people in the renewal of the covenant (see Joshua 8:34; 24:25; 2 Kings 23:2–3). It is noteworthy that Josiah was the one king to receive the unqualified approval of the Deuteronomists: 'Before him there was no king like him, who turned to the Lord with all his heart, with all his soul, and with all his might, according to all the law of Moses; nor did any like him arise after him' (2 Kings 23:25). For Christian readers of the story of Joshua, however, his name (meaning 'the Lord is salvation') will resonate above all with that of the later Joshua, or Jesus, the servant of God who offers God's deliverance not merely from earthly enemies, and leads those who will follow into God's fuller presence. Frances Ridley Havergal's hymn re-echoes the challenge of Joshua and invites us to make the appropriate commitment.

Who is on the Lord's side?
Who will serve the king?
Who will be his helpers
Other lives to bring? ...

We are on the Lord's side;
Saviour, we are thine.

FURTHER READING

A. Graeme Auld, *Joshua, Judges & Ruth* (The Daily Study Bible), St Andrew Press, 1984. An excellent little commentary, which combines attention to the original context and the message for today.

Trent C. Butler, *Joshua* (Word Biblical Commentary), Word Books, 1983. A very detailed commentary, with detailed bibliographies, in a rather conservative series.

Adrian H.W. Curtis, *Joshua* (Old Testament Guides), Sheffield Academic Press, 1994. An introductory guide to the book of Joshua.

David M. Gunn, 'Joshua and Judges' in R. Alter and F. Kermode (eds), *A Literary Guide to the Bible*, Collins, 1987. A useful literary approach to the book of Joshua.

Carolyn Pressler, *Joshua, Judges and Ruth* (Westminster Bible Companion), Westminster John Knox Press, 2002. A useful commentary, which addresses issues of original context and meaning for today.

MARK 12—16

Our last set of studies covered the second 'act' of Mark's drama, which narrated Jesus' journey to Jerusalem with his disciples (8:22—10:52), and then took us into the dramatic opening of the third act with Jesus' conspicuous (one might almost say flamboyant) arrival outside the city as the messianic king, followed by his startling attack on the temple régime. This challenging arrival set the scene for a direct confrontation between Jesus and the Sanhedrin authorities, and our studies finished with Jesus' veiled but unmistakable attack on their position in the parable of the vineyard (12:1–12).

Now a series of question-and-answer encounters with a variety of influential groups (12:13–37) leads up to Jesus' final denunciation of both the scribes and the temple authorities in 12:38–44, after which he abandons the temple and predicts its coming destruction. This leads into a long section of teaching given to Jesus' disciples about what the future holds (13:3–37).

The stage is thus set for the story to reach its climax, as the authorities, with the help of Judas, finally get Jesus into their power. The story of his arrest, trial and condemnation takes its inexorable course, but Mark will keep reminding us that all this is not because Jesus has been defeated, but because this was his God-given mission all the time. Even when Jesus is crucified, there will be a paradoxical blend of powerlessness and purpose, and, behind the mocking titles conferred on Jesus by the soldiers, the authorities and the crowds, we shall be invited to recognize his true identity as the king on the cross.

Jesus' repeated predictions of his death ever since 8:31 have also mentioned resurrection. He has prepared his disciples to meet him again in Galilee. But when we read at last of the discovery of the empty tomb, the story will suddenly stop short, with the message undelivered and the planned meeting not recorded. Modern scholars are virtually unanimous that 16:8 is the end of Mark's text as it has come down to us, and that 16:9–20 is a well-meaning but rather clumsy attempt by second-century Christians to fill the perceived gap. Many argue that Mark intended to finish there, deliberately leaving his readers to finish the story for themselves. Others think he intended to write more (as Matthew did in his otherwise similar ending) but either he failed to finish the book or his original ending was lost. See what you think when we get to the final study!

1 A political challenge

Mark 12:13–17

When Jesus was a boy, the Romans had imposed direct rule on Judea (unlike Galilee). The poll tax which they then imposed was an affront to Jewish national sentiment, and had sparked off a serious armed revolt. It remained a very sore point. But Jesus was a Galilean, so what did this distinguished teacher from another province think about their local political debate? It is posed as an innocent academic question, but of course neither response would be without danger. A 'yes' would immediately alienate Jesus from patriotic Judeans, while a 'no' could be used to portray him to the Romans as a trouble-maker, like Judas the Galilean who had led the poll tax revolt.

The silver denarius with which the tax must be paid bore an image of the emperor and an inscription describing him as 'Son of God'; to the Jews this was idolatrous, but the Romans met their scruples by allowing them to use local copper coinage for daily business. So Jesus' request for a denarius cut the ground from under their feet: he did not have one of these obnoxious Roman coins, but they did! Well, if they were using Caesar's currency, they could hardly object to paying his tax.

But Jesus' famous pronouncement goes further. The question assumed that there must always be a conflict between loyalty to God and obedience to a state that does not acknowledge him. Jesus denies this. It is possible to be both a loyal citizen and a consistent servant of God. There is not necessarily a choice to be made between the two. Of course there may be times when Caesar sets himself against God, as Christians were to discover before very long, and then there will be difficult choices to be made. But that situation, Jesus suggests, is not the norm.

101

It is a clever answer, in that it neatly avoids the 'yes/no' dilemma posed by the original question. It presumably approves the payment of the tax in normal circumstances, but in a way that avoids making it a religious issue. But it also provides a more wholesome model for reflection on Christian citizenship than their unthinking assumption that the state is inherently against God.

2 A question about life after death

Mark 12:18–27

The Sadducees controlled the temple and supplied most of its priests. They have come to poke fun at the new-fangled idea, adopted by their opponents the Pharisees (and, they assume, also by Jesus), that there is life after death. They base their question on the law of Deuteronomy 25:5–6, which provided 'immortality' for someone who died childless, by means of surrogate parenthood. If death is not the end, doesn't that pose a problem for the woman who has had a series of husbands before death?

It is meant as a cynical put-down, but in fact it raises a serious issue for those who, unlike the Sadducees, do believe in life after death—especially in these days when multiple marriages are an increasingly common experience. So Jesus tackles it seriously. The Sadducees' problem is that they assume that life after death, if it exists, will be just like a continuation of this life. But marriage as we know it belongs to this world with its family structures and the need to produce children. In eternity it will be different; the exclusiveness of the marriage relationship will not apply in heaven.

Underlying the cynical question, however, was the more fundamental issue of whether death is really the end. Jesus' 'proof' of the resurrection in verses 26–27 is so terse as to be quite cryptic. His point seems to be that Abraham, Isaac and Jacob had long been dead when God identified himself to Moses as *their* God (Exodus 3:6). If he is still 'their' God several centuries later, they cannot be really dead. When God identifies himself as 'the God of...' this is the language of covenant, and God had made a covenant for ever with Abraham and his family. How can God's covenant simply evaporate when the person with whom he made it dies?

The eternal God makes eternal covenants, and so the relationship cannot be cut short by death. That seems to be the gist of the argument. It is drawn from a text in the law of Moses because that is the only part of the Old Testament that the Sadducees regarded as fully authoritative. There are, of course, much clearer evidences of life after death in the prophets and the psalms.

3 Two more questions

Mark 12:28–37

The final question addressed to Jesus comes from a man who is apparently not ill-disposed towards him, although the request to single out one central commandment from all the 613 commandments in the law of Moses is one that might be expected to trigger strong disagreements. The rabbis sometimes discussed the question, and several different proposals are recorded in their traditions. Jesus chooses not one but two commands, which between them sum up the two main thrusts of the Ten Commandments—our duty to God and to other people. But the texts he chooses speak not of duty but of love. This goes to the heart of the matter, our essential attitudes and loyalties, not simply a code of rules to be followed.

If a fundamental principle is to be singled out, it would be hard to fault Jesus' choice, and the questioner is satisfied. After so often reading about scribes as Jesus' opponents (as we will again in 12:38–40), it is refreshing to meet one of them who is willing to give his approval where it is deserved. Jesus' comment that this man is 'not far from the kingdom of God' (v. 34) suggests that he is a potential disciple (like Joseph of Arimathaea, 15:43), but we have no way of knowing what happened to him after this meeting.

Now it is Jesus' turn to pose a theological question. It is worded without reference to his own status, and he has not yet made in public an explicit claim to be the Messiah, although those who saw him ride to the city on the donkey could hardly have missed the point. But what sounds like an academic question has obvious relevance to what people are saying about Jesus himself. 'Son of David' was a recognized title for the coming Messiah (see its use in 10:47–48), so Jesus' argument is surprising. Is he denying this basic scriptural theme? More probably, he is pointing out that 'Son of David', if it implies someone who is no more than just another David, is too weak a term for what God has promised—David's *lord*. The argument is left tantalizingly open-ended, but it allows the Christian reader to reflect that Jesus is revealed in this Gospel not as son of David but as Son of God.

4 Judgment on the temple

Mark 12:38—13:2

The brief comment on the scribes in verses 38–40 seems mild compared with the long diatribe in Matthew 23. But it highlights two failings, which together add up to a dangerous cocktail: an over-inflated sense of their own importance, and an unscrupulous attitude to those who ought to be able to depend on their support. This is what Matthew calls 'hypocrisy'. Pompousness alone might be excused as a natural human failing, but they are also misusing their privileged position. We can only speculate on just how they 'devoured widows' houses' (excessive fees, mismanagement of their affairs, or misappropriation of assets entrusted to them?), but to exploit the most vulnerable and dependent members of society is despicable. To do it under a cloak of piety is unforgivable.

One of those exploited widows comes to our attention in the next scene, where Jesus and his disciples join the crowd who regularly gathered in the Court of the Women to watch people publicly tossing their gifts into the prominent collecting-boxes. Jesus' favourable comparison of the widow's tiny but costly gift with the painless largesse of the wealthy is typical of his radical comments on conventional values (see especially in chapter 10): the last are first and the first last. But it is probably significant also that this is the last episode set in the temple. Even here, at what should be the heart of the service of God, people are more concerned to gain a reputation for generosity than to help a poor widow.

With that, Jesus abandons the temple. One of his disciples, a typical Galilean tourist, is over-awed by Herod's magnificent complex of buildings (v. 1), but all Jesus can see is that it has failed as a place of worship (see 11:17). Like a few bold prophets before him (see Jeremiah 26), he even dares to declare that it is not inviolable. God has no further use for a building, however magnificent, that has become a focus for false worship and arrogant complacency: 'Not one stone will be left here upon another' (v. 2). As we now know, his prediction was literally true: a generation later, the Romans under Titus would destroy Herod's beautiful temple so completely that all we can now see of its 'massive stones' is a part of the substructure. Of the temple itself, nothing was left.

5 Hard times ahead

Mark 13:3–13

The disciples' question is in response to what Jesus has just said about the temple in 13:2. Many interpreters think that Jesus changed the subject and talked instead about his second coming, but I disagree. Up to 13:31, as I understand this discourse, Jesus is answering the disciples' question. It is all about what will happen to Jerusalem, and it will all happen within that generation (13:30). Only in 13:32, when he begins to speak of a specific 'day and hour' which remains unknown, does he apparently move on to speak of more ultimate events. Since this differs from many people's understanding of the discourse, I thought I ought to warn you at the beginning!

The next 30-odd years would be a turbulent time in Jewish history, and Jesus warns his disciples against seeing every disastrous event as a sign of the end. Life will continue, and they must not panic too soon. In particular, they can expect messianic pretenders to take advantage of the troubled times, but they are not to be deceived. This is not yet the end of Jerusalem, only the 'beginning of birth pains' (v. 8).

During this unsettled period, Jesus' disciples can expect to be singled out for hostile attention. People will remember that their leader had dared to predict the destruction of the temple. Once Jesus himself has been executed as a false messiah and as a danger to national morale, those who are still loyal to him will be branded as unpatriotic and a threat to national security. So Jesus prepares them by pointing out that this will be an opportunity for 'witness' (v. 9) to the truth they have learnt, and for the good news of the kingdom of God to go out not only to Jews but into the wider world (as indeed happened, especially through the work of the apostle Paul). Far from being cowed by official hostility, they are to trust God to give them the words to speak. Verses 9–11 almost read as a summary of the story of the post-Easter church as we read it in Acts.

It will be a testing time for the disciples, but God will see them through it. Eventually things will come to their climax, as Jesus has predicted—and as we shall see in the next study.

6 The end of the old order

Mark 13:14–27

The 'abomination that causes desolation' which heralds the approaching disaster is, in Daniel's prophecy, a term for the desecration of the temple by the pagan king Antiochus (Daniel 11:31; 12:11). Scholars dispute what actual event Jesus had in mind when he used Daniel's phrase, but in some way it will be obvious that the time has now come to escape before it is too late. Anyone who has read Josephus' graphic description of the siege of Jerusalem and its eventual capture in AD69–70 will realize that verses 17–20 do not exaggerate the horrors of the actual situation. Even then, perhaps especially then, there will be impostors who exploit the public anxiety, but Jesus' disciples are forewarned and need not be duped by them.

Note that the vivid language of verses 24–27 is not said to relate to some other event far in the future (Jesus' second coming), but to what will occur 'in those days'. People instinctively read this language of cosmic disruption as describing the end of the world, but Jesus is echoing the language of the Old Testament prophets, who used cosmic imagery to describe catastrophic events within earthly history, especially the destruction of great empires (see Isaiah 13:10; 34:4, from which most of the phrases in verses 24–25 are taken). And when, in verse 26, we read of the Son of Man 'coming', the word is not the technical term for the second coming, *parousia*, but echoes Daniel's vision of 'one like a son of man' who 'comes' before God's throne in heaven (not to earth) to receive kingship for ever (Daniel 7:13–14). This is the language of enthronement. So when eventually Jerusalem is taken and the temple destroyed, the old régime will be finished, and Jesus, the Son of Man, will be vindicated and enthroned as king for ever. The angels will gather people from all nations into his kingdom, and so the kingdom of God will be established under its divinely appointed sovereign, the Son of Man.

All this will happen, says Jesus, within this generation (v. 30). The end of the temple will finally confirm that God has instead set up his ultimate kingdom in which people of all nations will worship him as he deserves.

Guidelines

The temple has been the focus of this week's readings, first as the location of Jesus' teaching and debates, and then as the object of his condemnation (as already seen in 11:15–17) and his prophetic words. Note how the issue will be raised again in 14:58 and 15:29, 38, and see the continuing fall-out in Acts 6:13–14.

Think about the impact of Jesus' attitude on:

- ordinary people in Jerusalem, for whom it was axiomatic that the temple was the focus of God's presence among his people, as well as the pride and joy of their city and nation.
- Jesus' Galilean disciples, especially the four who heard his words on the Mount of Olives.

What does all this teach us about the nature of God's presence among his people, and about the dangers of a formal religious establishment?

1 Looking further into the future

Mark 13:28–37

Jesus has just spoken (on my understanding of this controversial chapter) in highly coloured terms about the coming destruction of the temple. The disciples had asked him when it would happen and what sign would herald it (13:4). In verses 28–31 he sums up his answer to that question.

Just as the sprouting of fig leaves is a sure sign of the arrival of summer, so the events he has spoken of in the siege of Jerusalem will herald the temple's destruction. As for when it will be, he is quite unequivocal: it will be within that generation. Remember his words in 9:1 about some who are then alive not dying before they see that the kingdom of God has come in power. The mustard seed will have grown, and the kingdom of God will be visibly established, while some of them are still alive. What will happen to the temple is the flipside of that coin. They can trust Jesus' words, for they, like the words of God, will never prove false. And they didn't!

But in verse 32 the language changes. What is this 'day and hour' (terms not used in the discourse so far) which, unlike the carefully dated destruction of the temple, is not known even to Jesus himself? He does not say in so many words, but in the light of similar language in the other Gospels (and especially in Matthew, who greatly expands this section into a series of parables about what he now describes as the *parousia*: 24:36—25:46) I think it most likely that Jesus has now moved on from the catastrophic events within history which have been his subject so far, to talk also about the end of history, when the kingship of the Son of Man declared in verse 26 will reach its final consummation. (This was not part of the disciples' question as Mark phrased it, though Matthew 24:3 has made it so.) The call to remain alert does not end with the events of AD70; God's people must always remain ready also for their Lord's return. If he himself could not tell them when it would be, how much less can they hope to work it out for themselves. Just be ready!

2 Getting ready for Passover

Mark 14:1–16

The central point of the Passover festival was the formal family meal, celebrated in homes; in Jesus' case, his group of disciples takes the place of family (cf. 3:34–35). But this is no ordinary Passover. Jesus knows that his time is running out, and he plans to make this an extra special meal. The careful instructions to his disciples, and the availability of a large room in the crowded city, suggest that Jesus had already planned this event with the help of a sympathizer who lived in Jerusalem.

The note of urgency is underlined by verses 1–2 and 10–11. We already knew about the authorities' hostility to Jesus, but they now find an unexpected ally in one of the Twelve. We can only speculate as to what motivated Judas to change sides. Few believe that the payment alone was enough to make him abandon the cause to which he had devoted so many months. He must have concluded for some reason that Jesus really was wrong. Was it perhaps Jesus' attack on the temple that turned him? We shall never know.

Set within this threatening scenario is the surprising story of an unnamed woman's uncalculating devotion. To others it was waste; to her it was a proper recognition of who Jesus was. It all depends on your priorities, and by taking her side against the more hard-headed disciples Jesus puts spontaneous devotion above even well-motivated economy. Of course, if we pushed that principle to its logical extreme, responsible living and especially prudent church finances would become impossible, but Jesus does not say that the poor must *always* take second place. Rather, this is a special occasion, when even their undoubted claim on his people's generosity might appropriately be postponed.

Mark does not say that the woman intended her spontaneous gesture as a burial anointing. It is Jesus, knowing what is in store for him, who sees it in that extra light (note that the anointing which should normally accompany his burial will come too late: 16:1). Because of that special significance, she will be honoured wherever the good news is preached.

Her story will be told, but her name will not be recorded! In the kingdom of God, what we do counts for more than who we are.

3 A Passover meal with a difference

Mark 14:17–25

John's Gospel gives us five whole chapters about this special farewell meal, but Mark records only two key episodes from it.

First, Jesus has not been taken by surprise by Judas' change of side, and now he tries to prepare the rest of the Twelve for this body-blow. Their rather pathetic response, 'Surely not I?', shows a realistic awareness of the human weakness that they have all displayed too often on the way to Jerusalem. But their reaction also indicates that Judas has kept his intentions secret from everyone except Jesus, and Jesus does not identify him. If he had, it is doubtful that Judas would have been allowed to leave the room alive, and Jesus knows that Judas' betrayal is part of the total course of events that must take place according to scripture (14:49).

The Passover meal contained ritual explanations of the courses of food and cups of wine, recalling aspects of Israel's original deliverance from Egypt. Within that context of redemption, Jesus adds his own staggering new symbolism. The bread and wine now represent his own body and blood, soon to be given for the redemption not only of these few disciples but 'for many'. The original Passover was marked by the death of lambs, sacrificed to bring deliverance to Israel when the firstborn of Egypt were killed; now a new sacrifice is to take place, for the deliverance of 'many'. Following that original exodus, God made a covenant with his people, sealed with the blood of sacrifices; now Jesus' blood seals a new covenant, setting up a new people of God. This is nothing less than the rebirth of Israel.

The disciples ate the bread and drank the wine. Symbolically they were participating in Jesus' saving death. They were the founding fathers of the new people of God.

As the significance of Jesus' words gradually dawned on them, the disciples could no longer avoid the uncomfortable truth. He had said he was coming to Jerusalem to die, and now he was enacting that death symbolically before them. Soon it would happen for real. But he had also talked about resurrection, however little they had understood it, and now again he looks beyond death and burial to the new life in the kingdom of God. Jesus' next meal will be in glory.

4 Gethsemane

Mark 14:26–42

Judas has gone about his business, and Jesus and the remaining eleven disciples go out to the place where they have been in the habit of meeting during this week. As they go, Jesus warns them of danger and failure ahead, but again the ominous prediction is balanced by resurrection and a glimpse of a future beyond the disaster. For now, however, the immediate danger fills the horizon. The disciples' confident protestations of loyalty will be short-lived (see 14:50), and Peter's, which is the loudest, will be the most comprehensively disproved (14:66–72).

Already, when they get to Gethsemane, the disciples' weakness is only too clear: they can't even stay awake for him when he needs them. When Jesus speaks of weakness of the flesh (v. 38), however, he is referring not just to ordinary tiredness, but to a more fundamental lack of stamina and determination for what lies ahead. If they cannot stay awake and pray, they are not going to be able to face the test. So when the crisis arrives, they will be caught napping—both literally and in terms of their spiritual preparedness.

Jesus' own preparation for his ordeal is therefore even more lonely than it need have been. Mark's language indicates a deep emotional revulsion at what he is facing. Even after all the clear predictions of his suffering and death, and his own explicit enactment of it in the symbols of bread and wine, Jesus has to face his own 'weakness of the flesh'. He knows what he would prefer, and it conflicts with what he has come to understand is God's will for him. And so his prayer is a remarkable blend of honest entreaty and loyal acceptance of what he most fears. He needs to know that there is no other way, that even God, to whom everything is possible, has no Plan B. Once he is assured of that, his own will is loyally submitted to his Father's.

The familiar address to God as 'Abba' (the normal Aramaic term used by a son to his father) expresses the relationship that makes such a prayer possible. When, on the cross, Jesus says not 'Father' but simply 'my God', it will express poignantly the strain under which that relationship has been placed. That is what Jesus had to face up to in Gethsemane.

5 'Into the hands of sinners'

Mark 14:43–54

The priests recruited Judas to fulfil two functions: first, to guide the arresting party to the right group among the many thousands of Passover pilgrims camping out around Jerusalem in the festival week, and second, to identify Jesus (in the dark) among a group of unfamiliar Galileans. The first task was easy, since Jesus did not, as he could easily have done, give them the slip by choosing a different place to meet that evening. The second task was the reason for the infamous kiss.

Jesus is expecting them (14:41–42), but the disciples, still half asleep, panic. One briefly offers violent resistance, but it is futile, since Jesus makes it clear that he does not intend to resist arrest. He even pours scorn on mob's method of arresting him, at night on the hillside and with an armed posse rather than in broad daylight in the Court of the Gentiles. Did they really think he was going to fight back? Of course, it was not so much Jesus himself they were afraid of, but the volatile Passover crowd, at least some of whom would have been likely to take Jesus' side, and it could have become nasty (see 14:1–2). But here on the dark hillside, there was no contest.

Jesus seems determined to let things take their scripturally ordained course, and so the disciples lose any courage that they might have summoned up. They all abandon him, just as he has predicted. The curious story of the young man who ran away naked (often thought to be Mark himself, though he doesn't say so) simply underlines the completeness of the desertion. Jesus is entirely 'in the hands of sinners' (14:41).

So the scene is set at the high priest's house, with the whole member-ship of the Sanhedrin gathered to give Jesus a trial, of a sort. But out in the courtyard is Peter, the one disciple who, true to his boast (14:29), has got over his fear and followed behind the arresting posse. Mark thus sets up a double stage, and invites us to compare the way the two protagonists will respond under pressure, Jesus in the courtroom with the whole official establishment ranged against him, Peter incognito among a bunch of underlings. It will be a telling but ultimately dismal comparison.

6 'Are you the Messiah?' … 'I am!'

Mark 14:55–65

Mark's wording does not suggest an impartial trial, but due process must still be observed, and so the witnesses are called. The only accusation specifically recorded is a very telling one: Jesus has threatened the temple (v. 58). Even if he did not say the actual words quoted ('I will destroy'; cf. 13:2), the charge was near enough to the truth to be damaging, and it would not be forgotten (see 15:29). But Mark's phrasing of the charge adds a theological dimension that they could hardly have grasped at the time: the temple to be destroyed is a man-made one, but it will be replaced by a spiritual temple. The New Testament writers will delight to explore this idea (see 1 Corinthians 3:16–17; 1 Peter 2:5).

After the various witnesses have failed under cross-examination, the high priest decides on a direct approach. He has been well briefed (by Judas?) on what Jesus is understood to be claiming about his own status and mission. So, is it true? 'Are you the Messiah, the Son of God?' (v. 61). Jesus' reply is magnificently bold. No need any longer for secrecy; this is the moment of truth, with the highest authorities in the land as audience: 'I am!'

But he does not leave it at that. His words blend the scriptural images of the enthroned Son of Man (Daniel 7:13–14; cf. Mark 8:38; 13:26) and the Messiah at God's right hand (Psalm 110:1; cf. Mark 12:35–37). As in 13:26, this is not the 'coming' of Jesus' ultimate return, but his presentation before God in heaven. He, the prisoner in the dock, is soon to be seated in heavenly authority and glory—so soon that they themselves will see it (remember how, in 8:38—9:1 and in 13:26, Jesus has also spoken of his coming authority being revealed within that generation).

That is enough for the high priest. For this miserable prisoner to claim to be enthroned as God's Son is not only ludicrous but also blasphemous —unless, of course, it is true, and that possibility does not seem to be considered. The Sanhedrin agree, the death penalty is approved, and the formal judicial hearing degenerates into rowdy mockery and physical abuse, as each outdoes the others in proving his revulsion at such blasphemy.

Guidelines

Put yourself in the place of the various actors in the drama of chapter 14. What would you have made of it all?

- The chief priests, in their plotting and their eventual 'triumph'.
- Judas, in his agreement with the priests, at the Passover meal, and in Gethsemane.
- The woman who anointed Jesus.
- The disciples listening to Jesus' words at the meal, sleeping in Gethsemane, running away.

- The mysterious young man who ran away naked.
- The guards who arrested Jesus and then gathered in the high priest's courtyard.
- Peter, as he dares to follow Jesus (and in his own moment in the spotlight: see next week).

Perhaps it is too bold to try to put ourselves also in Jesus' place. But how do you respond to the various things he has said and done and experienced in this chapter?

1 Meanwhile, out in the courtyard
Mark 14:66–72

While Jesus has been facing hostile interrogation inside the house, Peter is hoping to avoid being noticed out in the courtyard. But sitting by the fire was not a good idea, and his face is visible in the firelight. It is obvious that he doesn't belong. Notice the terms 'Nazarene' and 'Galilean': Peter stands out as a stranger, like the man on trial, and when he speaks his Galilean accent gives the game away (see Matthew 26:73).

The three challenges to Peter are in ascending order of seriousness. First there is just a single servant-girl; then she appeals to others to confirm her allegation; finally the whole group of people around him join in the charge. Three challenges bring out three denials, just as Jesus had said (14:30), and those denials also increase in strength as the accusation becomes more difficult to parry. The first two are met with a simple denial, though that in itself is serious enough in the light of Peter's promise never to disown Jesus (14:31). But the third time Peter resorts to an oath. It is possible that this means simply that he swore that his statement was true ('May God do so-and-so to me if…'), but the Greek word Mark uses refers elsewhere to a curse on someone else, not on oneself, and he may well mean that Peter even went so far as to curse Jesus, in order to prove he was not his follower. This, according to the Roman governor Pliny, is what the Roman authorities later required people accused of being Christians to curse Jesus in order to prove their innocence.

If so, Peter's capitulation could not be more complete. His breakdown when the cock-crow reminds him of Jesus' prediction is one of utter self-disgust. His boasted loyalty has evaporated into abject surrender.

That could have been the end of the story of Peter. He will not appear again in Mark's narrative, but in 16:7 the message to the disciples is addressed also (especially?) to Peter; he has not been given up, and his subsequent history will show that even the most abject failure need not be terminal.

2 The Roman governor gets involved

Mark 15:1–15

Under Jewish law, blasphemy was a capital offence, but under the Roman occupation the Sanhedrin did not have the right to carry out the death penalty. So the Sanhedrin leaders had to find a way to get the Roman prefect, Pontius Pilate, to approve the execution. They decided to give Jesus' messianic claims a suitably political twist by using the phrase 'king of the Jews'.

Jesus' reply to the charge in verse 2 is not a straight yes or no. It probably means something like 'Yes, but not in the sense you have in mind.' Pilate seems to have sensed pretty quickly that any 'kingship' Jesus may have claimed was not of the sort to threaten Roman control, and so he tried to find a way out of the situation without provoking the Jewish leaders, with whom he was on rather delicate terms.

The way he chose, however, was not very clever. Invoking the custom of a festival amnesty, he offered the crowd a choice between two supposedly popular leaders, but his ignorance of Jewish culture and politics meant that it was not a real choice at all; it was a foregone conclusion. Barabbas was apparently a genuinely popular figure, arrested because of his leadership in an attempted patriotic uprising, which would put the Jerusalem populace firmly on his side. Jesus, however, was a stranger in Jerusalem, not one of their own, and the fact that their own religious leaders had rejected his claim and condemned him for blasphemy was enough to turn the people of the city against him. In stark contrast to the Galilean crowd who had shouted 'Hosanna' outside the city a few days earlier, the people of Jerusalem shouted, 'Crucify him!' (v. 13).

Pilate was a bully, and not a strong man of principle. He was not prepared to risk public order for the sake of a village preacher, however innocent he may have thought him to be. Barabbas, the would-be political leader, was released while the non-political 'king of the Jews' was condemned to die instead.

Crucifixion was a vicious Roman form of execution reserved normally for slaves and political rebels. It was regularly accompanied by flogging, a savage punishment that often left people half-dead even before they went to the cross. By the time Jesus was taken out by the soldiers, he would already have been in a pitiful state.

3 Crucifixion

Mark 15:16–32

In this passage, brutality and mockery are combined. The Roman soldiers' horse-play was rough, but it was also savagely ironical. As far as they were concerned, this 'king of the Jews' was a failed rebel against Rome, and they made the most of their opportunity to humiliate him in a mock coronation.

Normally the victim himself was forced to carry the heavy crossbeam to which he was to be fixed when it was slotted into the upright at the place of execution. Jesus is apparently already too much weakened by flogging and torture to do so, and a complete stranger is commandeered instead. It is striking that Mark mentions his sons' names (v. 21), as if he expects his readers to know them: did the family become disciples as a result of this experience?

The crucifixion took its normal course, in a familiar place of execution and carried out by soldiers used to the routine. The offer of a pain-killing drink may have come from well-wishers rather than from the soldiers themselves, but Jesus refused it perhaps because he was determined to go through the awful experience in full consciousness. The placard on the cross summed up his supposed political crime, and the placing of two of Barabbas' colleagues on either side added to the irony.

Mark's readers, who knew about Roman crucifixion, would have had no illusions about the sheer physical agony involved in hoisting a man up on the cross. But Mark's account of the crucifixion focuses less on the pain than on the psychological torture of the mockery from the passing crowds, the Sanhedrin authorities, and even Jesus' fellow sufferers on the other crosses.

As we listen to their taunts, though, we realize that what they meant in jest was in fact the truth about the Jesus we have come to know. He *is* a king; he *is* going to replace the temple; he *does* save others; he *is* the Messiah, the king of Israel. But all this is true on a level far removed from what these mockers are thinking of. Indeed, his dying on the cross is itself the means of fulfilling his mission and saving others (see 10:45; 14:24). It is precisely because he is the saviour of others that he cannot come down from the cross.

4 The death of Jesus

Mark 15:33–39

Since Jesus' cryptic reply to Pilate in 15:2, we have heard no word from his lips. He has been passive in the hands of his enemies. But now, after hours of agony, he breaks his silence in a tremendous and disturbing shout.

His words are the opening words of Psalm 22, a psalm of suffering that has been subtly echoed already in Mark's narrative in 15:24 and 29 (see Psalm 22:18 and 22:7 respectively). But surely Jesus is not just reciting a familiar text: the psalm expresses his own desperate sense of abandonment. This is the only time we hear of Jesus addressing God as anything but 'Father'. Something drastic has happened to their relationship. For a time (and Luke 23:46 encourages us to believe that it was only for a time), Jesus, the Son of God, feels himself cut off from his Father. Later theologians have explained that Jesus was bearing the weight of human sin and that it was this that came between Father and Son. Mark, however, does not explain it; he simply allows us to share the agony of Jesus' desolation.

The mishearing of his cry as an appeal to Elijah (who was popularly expected to come to help God's people in dire need) provides an almost comic interlude, but soon the end comes—surprisingly soon for those who were used to crucifixions, which usually resulted in the victims lingering on in agony for many hours, or even days.

Jesus' death is marked by two extraordinary happenings. First is the tearing of the temple curtain (v. 38, probably the one that closed the entrance to the sanctuary where the priests carried out their sacred duties). It was a huge, sumptuous piece of tapestry, over 80 feet high according to Josephus. For it to be torn from top to bottom implies a non-human agency. Here is a symbol of the judgment on the temple that Jesus has predicted. The way into the presence of God is thrown open, and the priestly monopoly ended.

The other striking event is the 'confession' of the centurion, the first and only observer in this Gospel to state what God had declared at the beginning, that Jesus was God's Son (v. 39). How much this meant theologically in the mouth of a Roman may be debated, but Mark's readers cannot fail to appreciate the point. The truth is out.

5 Dead and buried

Mark 15:40–47

The male disciples have all run away. Now the women, who have been a silent presence throughout Jesus' ministry, come into their own. It is they who provide the vital continuity of witness, watching his death and his burial, and then finding the same tomb left empty. So there is no room for mistake.

Crucified bodies were not normally buried, but thrown out on the ground. Jewish piety was scandalized by this Roman practice, and it is possible that Joseph is doing no more here than any other pious Jew might do. But he seems to be interested in only one of the three bodies, and Mark's comment that he was 'waiting for the kingdom of God' (v. 43) suggests that he was at least a secret sympathizer with Jesus. Whether he was absent from the Sanhedrin when Jesus was tried, or was overruled, we cannot know. At least now he wants to make amends for what has been done, and takes the risky step of approaching Pilate, and so identifying himself with an executed criminal.

Pilate's surprise at the speed of Jesus' death is mentioned to avoid any suggestion that he had not really died; Pilate had it confirmed by the centurion, who was experienced enough to know when a crucified man was dead.

Joseph had to act quickly, as the body had to be buried before sunset, when the sabbath began; that is probably why, after the sabbath, the women will come to anoint the body, normally part of the burial ritual (16:1), although John 19:39–40 says that Joseph had in fact wrapped spices in with the burial clothes. Mark tells us that the tomb was cut in the rock, with a stone rolled against the door (like several that can still be seen around Jerusalem). Matthew adds that it was Joseph's own new tomb, and Luke and John underline that it had not yet been used. That is important, since rock-cut tombs were normally made to accommodate several bodies, but in this one there was no other body, and so no possibility of confusion when the space was later found to be empty.

So Jesus has been safely put away, confirmed dead and sealed in a rock tomb by a stone which three women cannot move (16:3). That looks like the end of the story.

6 'He has risen!'

Mark 16:1–8

The sabbath finished at sunset, 24 hours later, but it is early Sunday morning before anyone comes to the tomb; by Jewish inclusive time-reckoning, that makes it 'after three days' (e.g. 8:31) from the Friday evening burial, even though it was little more than 36 hours.

The women do not see Jesus rise from the dead; no one does, in any of the Gospel accounts. He has already gone when they get there and find the stone rolled away. Instead they find a 'young man' (v. 5). The other Gospels speak of one or more angels, and the 'white robe' is typical of accounts of angelic appearances, but perhaps the women were not sure just whom they had met. At any rate, the man is well-informed: he knows who they are and what they have come for, and, more important, he knows what has happened to Jesus. Moreover, he has a message for them, presumably from Jesus himself. It is for the remaining disciples, and it repeats what Jesus had told them himself before his death (14:28). The special mention of Peter is a warm pastoral touch, to assure the fallen disciple that even after his shameful failure, he is still included.

So far, so good. We might expect now to hear how the women delivered the message and the disciples went to Galilee and met the risen Jesus—but far from it. If verse 8 really is the end of Mark's Gospel (see the introduction to these notes), it seems to pull the rug out from under all that Mark has carefully constructed so far. They ran away and told no one: 'they were scared, you see'. What a way to finish the book! It leaves you waiting for the other shoe to drop.

This appeals to some modern literary taste, finishing on a note of mystery and challenge: they didn't pass on the message, so it's over to you, the readers! Early users of Mark didn't see it that way, and someone put together what we call Mark 16:9–20, largely cobbled together from extracts from the endings of the other Gospels. That, and an alternative 'shorter ending', soon circulated as part of Mark's text, even though he didn't write them. Personally, I too find it incredible that he meant to leave the book like that, with its promise unfulfilled. I suspect that Mark intended to, and probably did, go on to narrate the meeting in Galilee, just as Matthew, whose account is otherwise close to Mark's, did. If so, the original ending must have been lost, but no one knows how or when. It must remain a mystery.

Guidelines

Were you there when they crucified my Lord?
Sometimes it causes me to tremble, tremble, tremble.
Were you there when they crucified my Lord?

We weren't, and we can't be, but the story still moves people. A simple reading aloud of Mark's account of the crucifixion is still worth many long sermons on the doctrine of atonement.

Try reading it again, perhaps identifying yourself with one of those unsung women from Galilee whom we meet in 15:40–41 and who were spectators of it all.

We have the 'advantage' over them of centuries of debate about just how Jesus' death secures the world's salvation. Do you think we really understand it better?

REVELATION 1—11

What is your instant reaction to the book of Revelation? 'Impenetrable and confusing'? Or maybe 'bloodthirsty and sub-Christian'? For many people it is simply unknown. The seven letters to the churches in chapters 2 and 3 are familiar, often used as a series for sermons or Bible studies. Similarly, the vision at the beginning of chapter 21 of a new heaven and a new earth in which 'death will be no more; mourning and crying and pain will be no more' provides comfort in many funerals. Other snippets are recognizable, particularly because of the influence of Revelation on art and music: the lamb that had been slain (ch. 5), the two beasts (ch. 13), the 'whore of Babylon' (chs 17—18). In general, though, it is a foreign country, and many of those who seem to spend a lot of time there are not its best advocates, often appearing extreme, unbalanced or fanatical.

This is a great shame. God did not give the book of Revelation to the church by mistake. All of God's gifts are designed to bring about the good, to work for the benefit of humanity. All, though, can be misused and distorted. Revelation does not belong to extremist cults and fanatics any more than sex belongs to the 'sex industry': if it appears so, that is only because the church has given up on it because it is too strange. Over the next two issues of *Guidelines* we will begin to explore this fascinating foreign country, and come to understand its logic, its structures and its message. We will find that much of its foreignness is only skin-deep: familiar concerns, hopes and fears are expressed in a different language and through different customs.

Our study has three aims. First, simply that you would gain an understanding of Revelation, so that at least it is a better-travelled foreign country. Second, that you would start to have some confidence that Revelation does belong in the Christian Bible, and not to extremists, and can perhaps share that confidence with others. Third, and most importantly, that you would hear God speaking through it: there is much here of direct relevance for us and our churches today.

Saying 'today' immediately raises a key question. 'Doesn't Revelation just speak about the end?' As soon as we stop and think about this, we realize how strange it would be if it did. Why would God give to his people

121

a book that was going to be of use only to one particular generation alive at one particular moment? Revelation is about exactly that—'revelation'. That is what the Greek word 'apocalypse' (the first word of the book) means. Despite how it is used in general conversation today, at the heart of an apocalypse is 'unveiling'—revealing the truth about the way the world 'is, was, and is to come' (to quote Revelation). The purpose of that unveiling is not to equip some future generation with a blueprint of events, but to equip Christians in every age with divine insight into their world.

1 Introduction

Revelation 1:1–8

The book opens with a clear statement of what it is: it contains what was revealed to John. Immediately we see the strong Christological ('Jesus-centred') nature of Revelation: yes, it is a revelation from God; yes, it came through an angel; but it is properly seen as the 'revelation of Jesus Christ'. Jesus is the one through whom God is revealed in the world. It is emphasized that this is not a message for the distant future. It is about things that 'must soon take place' for 'the time is near' (v. 3, cf. Mark 1:15). The period of waiting is over. This contrasts with other Jewish 'revelations' (apocalypses), which needed to be 'sealed up' because they contained messages for the future (e.g. Daniel 12:4, 9).

Much could be said about verses 4–7, but let us focus on three aspects: what we discover about Jesus, about ourselves, and about the world. Jesus is called 'the ruler of the kings of the earth' (v. 5). At times, as we read Revelation, we may think that it depicts a battle between 'heaven' and 'earth', between God and the wicked kings of the earth. But here, right at the start, we are reminded that 'the earth is the Lord's' (Psalm 24:1); Jesus is already its ruler. However bad things may look, however much it appears as if evil is triumphing, Jesus is actually already the 'ruler of the kings of the earth'.

We are described (vv. 5–6) as being loved, having been freed from our sins by Jesus' blood, (his death) and as 'a kingdom, priests serving his

God'. In this we can see the sequence at the heart of the Christian message. First we were loved—'while we still were sinners' (Romans 5:8). God's love for us is not the result of what we do. But we needed rescue: we could not escape from the effect of our sin ourselves. Jesus' death did something for us without which we would still be imprisoned. Now, we are a new unity (notice that together we are a 'kingdom'; we are not each a king), worshipping God directly, bringing others to him (as 'priests') (see Exodus 19:5–6; 1 Peter 2:9).

Verse 7 sets up an ambiguity that runs throughout the book regarding the world. The description of the tribes 'wailing' (or, more properly, 'mourning') is a quotation from Zechariah 12:10, but there it is followed by forgiveness (Zechariah 13:1). Matthew 24:30 implies that the 'mourning' happens because people recognize Jesus too late. Which will it be? Will the nations mourn with repentance, or wail when they realize the truth too late?

2 A vision of Jesus

Revelation 1:9–20

Who is John? The truth is, we don't know. It sounds as if he had been exiled to Patmos, an offshore island, which would suggest that he was a figure of some prominence. Yet he does not give any credentials. Perhaps this is because he was well known to the seven churches mentioned (all situated on the west coast of Turkey)—maybe their leader, or revered apostle or prophet. Or perhaps who he was didn't matter: he was merely the vehicle for Jesus' message. Does the identity of the speaker change the way we listen?

Seven is an important number within Revelation—indeed, in Jewish thought more generally—being seen as a symbol of completeness. John is instructed to send his record of what he saw to seven churches (v. 11). In the next two chapters we will see individual words to each. But is the message just for these seven? It seems not: the seven churches represent the Church as a whole, throughout time and space—just as much of Jesus' teaching was told in a particular context, or to a particular person, but transcends that context to speak to all contexts. The variety among these seven churches represents the variety found in the Church overall.

The vision of Jesus in verses 13–16 provides a good lesson in the visions in Revelation. Can you draw this picture? Many have tried. What does it look like to have a sword coming out of your mouth? Or is this a way of describing the power of his words (cf. Hebrews 4:12). Revelation often piles images up on one another in a way that cannot be drawn or logically pieced together: they emerge from their visual impact on John the visionary, not from the calculating mind of a scholar. The details of this picture bring together descriptions found elsewhere of divine messengers (e.g. Daniel 10:6) and of God himself (e.g. Daniel 7:9; Ezekiel 1:22–28, 43:2), while declaring him to be human (a son of man). Jesus is all three.

Notice where Jesus is said to be. Is he in heaven, perhaps waiting until he takes over the world at some future point? No, as we saw in 1:5, he already rules the world. He is 'in the midst of the lampstands' (v. 13), which are the churches (v. 20). Each of his messages in chapters 2 and 3 begin, 'I know…'. Jesus is present within the churches, if only they could see. If only we could see.

3 Letters to the Church (Part 1)

Revelation 2

This reading and the next one take in the seven letters to the churches. It is impossible to do each of them justice in so short a space, so we will focus on some overall themes. This also makes sense because, as we have said, these seven churches are in fact meant to represent the Church overall.

In each case, the message is said to be for 'the angel of the church'. Perhaps this is just a symbolic way of saying 'for the church'. However, it conveys an idea that we know is true, but is always hard to express. An organization, a group, is somehow more than its constituent parts. Thus, for example, the term 'institutional racism' has been coined to express a situation in which no individual is necessarily actively being racist, but overall the institution is. In other situations, one might talk of the need to change the 'culture' of an organization, which means not just the practices of particular individuals but something broader, the way in which the whole body functions. It is worth pausing to think what Jesus would say to the 'angel' of your church. Is your church critical, welcoming, insincere, dedicated, delusional or prayerful? The overall culture matters, as well as the activities of particular individuals.

The messages to each of the churches ends with a promise 'to everyone who conquers…', but what must they do in order to conquer? Of course there are some differences between the churches, but there is an overarching theme. The churches are praised for endurance, and they are warned about danger from deception. The deception comes in a variety of ways: false apostles (v. 2), slander (v. 9), teaching that causes people to stumble (v. 14), self-styled teachers and prophets who beguile the people (v. 20). Physical persecution is very limited: a forthcoming ten-day imprisonment for some (v. 10), and clearly, at some time in the past, a single martyrdom (v. 13). This theme will be continued throughout Revelation. The real danger to the Church does not come from naked outright attacks, but from deception, from the gradual absorption of practices and ideas contrary to the gospel. In this context we see what is distinctive about endurance: it is essentially passive, not active. But this passivity results in conquering because Jesus has already conquered, as we were reminded in the visions in chapter 1. The church does not need to go out and do a new work; it only has to remain faithful to the work that Jesus has already done. That way, it will share in his conquest.

4 Letters to the Church (Part 2)
Revelation 3

It is important to see how these messages to the seven churches connect to the rest of the book. Notice how the description of Jesus with which each message begins picks up an aspect of the description of Jesus from chapter 1. In this way, the seven form a complete message from the one Jesus. Notice also the promises made about 'those who conquer'. Take, for example, the white robes promised to those in Sardis (v. 5). Soon we will see humans seated in God's throne room dressed in white robes (4:4), and the image recurs frequently. Thus, as we read the rest of the book, we should remember the promise being held out to us, that we can become like the exalted, triumphant figures depicted later. But the key word here is 'can'. Revelation is often thought to portray the world in stark contrasts—goodies and baddies—but it is more subtle than that. In chapters 2 and 3 we have seen a very mixed, ambiguous portrayal of the Church. It is not portrayed simply as 'good' but as mixed (compare Matthew 13:24–30).

The rest of Revelation will use stark contrasts in depicting the world: good and evil. From God's perspective, there is good and evil, but what chapters 2 and 3 highlight is that you cannot equate good with the church—or, to put it another way, you cannot equate the visible church with God's people. Thus the word to the churches is '*if* you conquer'.

Thus we are alerted to two related but opposite dangers. Sometimes Christians can be guilty of arrogance, asserting that they know the truth, that they are 'pure'—in the language of Revelation, that they are already wearing 'white robes'. We can easily equate the 'goodies' depicted in the rest of Revelation with ourselves. But chapters 2 and 3 say 'no': the visible church—us—is far more mixed, and any note of conquest is proceeded by an 'if'. On the other hand, our society often seems to deny the concepts of 'good' and 'evil' entirely. Revelation says 'no': if only we could see the truth, we would see that there really is good and evil. Which error are you most susceptible to?

5 The throne in heaven

Revelation 4

A new vision begins. It is a vision that occurs 'after this' (v. 1): that is to say, John had the visions in chapters 1—3 before he had this vision. Here we learn an important lesson about the way in which Revelation is written. Many of the linking elements between passages, such as the words 'after this', are giving details about John's experience in having the visions; they do not tell us the sequence of the actual events themselves as depicted in the visions. John had the vision in chapter 4 after he had the vision in chapters 2 and 3, but this is very different from saying that the events in chapter 4 occur after the events in chapters 2 and 3. Indeed, chapter 4 really gives us a picture of God's *eternal* throne room. Just as God is outside time, chapter 4 is, in a sense, timeless. As we go from chapter to chapter, from vision to vision, we are often given different perspectives of the same 'events', not visions of sequential events. Worship was being offered in the heavenly throne room in chapter 4 long before John was born, continues today, and will go on long after I die.

Nevertheless, we should ask why the vision of chapter 4 follows the vision of chapters 2 and 3. Its effect is to reinforce the message about different perspectives. What we see when we look around us today is a situation similar to that in John's day, outlined in chapters 2 and 3: a church containing seemingly inseparable strands of good and evil, enduring to some extent, and being deceived in other ways. But God does not want us to think that what we see is how things actually are. With John we are lifted up to heaven to see that the real picture is different: in fact, God rules.

Notice also the population of the heavenly throne room (many of the details of this vision are paralleled in Ezekiel 1). The four 'living creatures' are a representation of the whole of the animal world. Alongside them are the elders, who are humans. Indeed, one of the 'living creatures' has a human face. The result is a depiction of humanity and the animals together in harmony, worshipping God. It is a bold vision for our age, when humans seem pitted against animals, wantonly destroying species and habitats. It is both a great comfort and a challenge to see that, in heaven, humans and animals will be together in harmony, praising their creator (v. 11).

6 The scroll and the lamb

Revelation 5

There is more. As John gazes at the heavenly scene of God worshipped as creator, he sees a drama being played out. There is a problem: there is a scroll in God's hand, but nobody can open it. The symbolism is clear: there is a message, a plan, of such overwhelming importance that it is depicted as lying in God's right hand in his throne room. But it cannot be brought about; nobody is worthy to open the scroll. This is very strange, for it suggests incompleteness, something important remaining to be done, something that cannot be done: hence John's tears.

Then John sees the lamb: there is, in fact, something in heaven that can open the scroll. This confounds expectations in many ways. The elder speaks of a conquering lion (v. 5), but John sees a lamb. The victor is depicted not as the most ferocious of animals, but as the most passive. What does that say about how victory is achieved? Furthermore, the lamb is 'standing as if it had been slaughtered' (v. 6). It is a butchered lamb, which, together with the later reference to blood (v. 9), highlights how victory was achieved through Jesus' death. Notice that even here in heaven, the lamb still bears the marks of his death: it was not a mistake or an embarrassment to be wiped out.

It is striking to suggest that God's creation (ch. 4) is in some way incomplete, that something more is needed. Chapter 5 gives the other half of the picture: salvation (particularly praised in verses 9–12). Completion comes from creation and salvation together, the one on the throne and the lamb (vv. 13–14). It is easy to emphasize one or the other—creation so much that salvation hardly seems necessary, or salvation so much that creation seems to be badly conceived and of little value.

Humans receive this work of salvation (vv. 9–10, echoing 1:5–6); we are not 'worthy' to bring about our own salvation. Furthermore, it is people 'from every tribe and language and people and nation' who are 'ransomed'. There is no cultural imperialism here: all nations and races are equally favoured by God.

Guidelines

This first quarter of Revelation has revealed to us the building blocks of a new perspective on our world. Its particular approach is to do this in bold language and imagery, and in contrasts. The effect is to challenge our 'grey' outlook, in which everything can be 'explained away' because it is 'complicated'. Of course life is complicated, but nevertheless how does it measure up? Four contrasts have been highlighted.

• First, heaven and earth: to us, reality seems to equate with earth. We tend to imagine that what we can see is all there is ('out of sight, out of mind'). The challenge is to remember that, in fact, God is reigning in his throne room now, with all creation worshipping him, and to live in the light of that vision.
• Second, creation and salvation: most of us focus on one or the other, but Revelation has shown us that creation is imperfect, salvation is needed, but creation itself is also good.

- Third, good and evil within the church: here we love to think that everything is 'OK', not brilliant but not bad. Revelation challenges us to be more perceptive and more honest. What in your local church is good, and what is bad? What would Jesus write to the angel of your church?
- Finally, the contrast set up in the first reading: will the nations mourn with repentance or wail when all is seen too late?

Revelation is a message from God to his servants. As you reflect on this week's readings, ask God to reveal to you his perspective on your world—your relationships, your work, your church, your spending of time and money—and commit yourself to changing how you live as a result of that insight.

1 The seals

Revelation 6

Here in chapter 6 we encounter the first of many descriptions of plagues and disasters, which give Revelation its unsavoury reputation. As we look at it carefully, though, there is much in this vision for future thought. It is far from depicting just 'a bloodthirsty God destroying his enemies'.

First notice the link to the previous chapter. What is depicted in this vision is said to accompany the opening of the seals on the scroll that the lamb took in chapter 5. That scroll was the plan or message of salvation. Here we learn that bringing about the plan involves pain and judgment as well. This is depressing, but sadly seems to fit with life around us. Good does not spread easily, and is not welcomed by all. Remember, though, that Revelation constantly depicts situations from multiple perspectives: here we are face to face with the negative, but chapter 7 brings a more positive view.

Judgment is a difficult topic. Christians are often divided: some seem to talk about nothing but judgment (normally judgment of others), while others never mention the word at all. But verses 9–11 highlight why judgment is necessary. Throughout the Bible, from the murder of Abel onwards, there is a consistent theme that innocent blood cries out to God (Genesis 4:10). Judgment is a necessary part of justice. The Bible asserts that God will avenge the weak, abused and powerless. Not surprisingly, it's a message that many of us find uncomfortable.

The sixth seal provides an important lesson in reading Revelation. Verses 12–14 describe events which can only be thought of as the end of the world, and yet the world continues to be depicted in chapters 7 onwards. This confirms our understanding that the sequence of visions does not depict the sequence of actual events, and the same events or situations can be portrayed many times in Revelation from different points of view. So in chapter 6 the end of the world is depicted, but it will be depicted again and again throughout Revelation.

The viewpoint here is the effect these judgments have on humanity, from the highest to the lowest. Sadly, it is negative. The judgments do not bring sinners to repentance; rather, people hide from God, just as Adam and Eve did in the garden (Genesis 3:10). The lamb is not wrathful, but the people think that he is. When people are alienated from God, a display of divine power will not bring them to repentance.

2 The great multitude

Soon we will return to plagues and judgments, but chapter 7 provides an interlude with its depiction of the 'sealing' of the servants of God, and the multitude in the heavenly throne room. Chapter 6 seems so negative, but chapter 7 is positive—the other side of the coin. The world as we experience it is a mixture of the two; Revelation highlights each in turn for us. Note, though, that the servants of God are marked with a seal for protection because they are going to live through the 'tribulation', the evil and suffering of our world (vv. 1–3, 14). This encapsulates an important truth: God promises protection but not comfort; ultimate security but not escape from suffering.

You may remember that in chapter 5 John was told of a triumphant lion of Judah, but what he saw was the slaughtered lamb. Here we have the same technique. What is heard is the expectation; what is seen is the wonderful fulfilment. The expectation is that a fixed number from Israel alone will be saved; the fulfilment is a countless multitude from every nation, tribe, people and language. God's mercy is far greater than we might expect. This speaks to us of the nature of God himself. We all know that our own salvation depends on God's mercy, yet our expectations are often that this mercy is quite limited—it has reached us but it won't reach many more.

The second half of this chapter gives us a 'glimpse of heaven'. Verses 9–14 seem to continue from chapter 5, with the depiction of the heavenly throne room and 'the one on the throne and the lamb' being praised for the salvation that has been brought. Verses 15–17 point in the other direction and echo many features of the depiction of the new heaven and new earth to be found in chapters 21—22. Thus Revelation reflects the line from the Lord's Prayer, 'your kingdom come, your will be done on earth as it is in heaven'. What is eternally true in the heavenly throne room will be true of the new heaven and the new earth, and is a key perspective to be balanced alongside the suffering that we see in our world. Now suffering and joy, judgment and salvation, chapter 6 and chapter 7, are interwoven, but one day 'God will wipe away every tear from their eyes' (v. 17).

3 The trumpets

Revelation 8

Revelation 8—9 contains a sequence of seven 'trumpets', paralleling in some fashion the 'seals' of chapter 6. Notice that, here, plagues affect a third of the earth, while in chapter 6 it was a quarter, which gives a sense of progression or intensification. As we have seen, the different visions within Revelation are not be taken as depicting a sequence of events, but rather the same situations from different perspectives, overlapping views and possibilities of our world. (Most obviously, what is said of the sun, moon and stars in verse 12 can hardly follow on from the events depicted in 6:12–14.) Nevertheless, Revelation asserts that all will not continue the same for ever. Positively, this is seen in the vision of the new heaven and the new earth: things will change. Negatively, we see it in the intensification of judgment: the end is approaching.

This is also a moment to consider how literally the visions should be taken. Should we think of a mountain literally being thrown into the sea (v. 8), or is this a poetic way of describing terrible events? In English we use the expression 'earth-shattering' to describe significant events, but we don't mean it literally. People in John's day were perfectly familiar with symbolic language. The truth is that we don't know, and perhaps it doesn't matter. I would take the language as accurately describing what John saw in his vision, but would suggest that the vision does not correspond directly to actual events: it is a way of depicting in striking images the truth about God, our world, and its future. But we should not fall into the trap of thinking that because it is not literal, it is meaningless. The electricity cable to my computer is not literally 'live', yet if I were to cut into it and hold the ends, I would not feel a 'symbolic' effect.

Notice the prayers of the saints in verse 4 (which also featured earlier, in the depiction of the heavenly throne room in 5:8). These visions seem dominated by God's plan, and by heavenly activity, yet in the midst of them we find human prayer. Prayer is always a conundrum: does God change his mind in response to our prayers? Revelation does not solve this puzzle but, along with the rest of the Bible, it insists both that God is in control and that our prayers are significant.

4 The end?

The consequence of the last three 'trumpets' is described in greater, lurid detail. This continues the effect of intensification, of the camera zooming in for the closing sequence. Some of the descriptions here draw on the particular context of John's day. In particular, the picture of the riders bringing destruction from east of the Euphrates comes from the political world of the first century AD, where the main enemies of the Roman empire were the Parthians east of the Euphrates, feared for their cavalry. Thus some features of the visions would have been particularly meaningful in John's day; the overall effect, however, remains clear.

Once again, Revelation is clear as to the effects of these judgments

(vv. 20–21; compare 6:15–17). One might think that judgment and the display of divine power would bring repentance and acknowledgment of God, but one of the insights of this part of Revelation is that this isn't true. All of God's power will not cause people to turn to him. In effect, we cannot force people to love us. In our own lives it is easy to fall into the trap of acting as if force, criticism and negativity bring about change. Of course truthfulness is important, but bullying and threats in the end achieve nothing.

Thus we come to a turning point in the book of Revelation. The outworking of the divine plan has been depicted in chapters 6—9, but it seems to fail, or at least have limited success. 'God's servants' are protected, and yet nothing good comes to the world as a whole. If we think back to the 'mourning' of the tribes in 1:7, it seems that, for all God's power, the 'mourning' will turn out to be people wailing when it is too late. God's plan does not seem to be 'good news'. Fortunately chapters 10 and 11 depict an alternative future. For now, though, we should ponder the message that force, negativity and criticism do not bring change. Often we act in our own lives, as churches and as nations, as if they can.

5 The mystery of God

Revelation 10

The last reading finished at a low point: power and judgments coming from heaven do not bring people to repentance. It seems as if all is lost as we await the seventh trumpet. But the trumpet does not sound. Instead John sees an angel carrying a scroll (vv. 1–2), linking us back to the scroll in chapter 5, which we thought was to bring salvation. The angel announces that 'the mystery of God' (v. 7) is about to be accomplished. All we have seen depicted has been negative, but it is not the whole story: there is a 'mystery', a 'secret plan', of God still to be unveiled.

The plan itself will be revealed in chapter 11, but now we note some features about how the plan ('the scroll') is enacted. Note that John is invited to take and eat the scroll. While, in chapter 5, it was clear that only the lamb was worthy to take the scroll, it appears that humans can then have a part in its outworking. We are not worthy to bring about God's plan, yet nevertheless he involves us in its execution.

The scene of the prophet eating the scroll reflects Ezekiel's commission in Ezekiel 2—3. This parallel reinforces the sense of the human (John) doing God's work, helping to bring about God's plan. An important contrast, though, is that Ezekiel was commissioned to speak to the people of Israel (Ezekiel 2:3), while John is told to speak to all people (v. 11): God's plan relates to all the peoples of the world. The idea of the prophet eating the scroll is a powerful image. God's message does not come to us as 'free-floating' words. At the heart of the Christian faith is the idea of the incarnation: 'the Word became flesh' (John 1:14). God's message comes to us lived out—primarily in the life of Jesus, and subsequently in the lives of his followers. The message reaches 'many peoples and nations and languages and kings' (v. 11) through the lives of people like John.

6 The witness of the Church

Revelation 11

Once again there is a symbolic partial protection of God's people (vv. 1–2): protection but no escape from suffering. Then we are introduced to the 'two witnesses' (v. 3). These symbolically represent God's people (the olive trees draw on Zechariah 4:1–7, we have already lampstands in chapter 1 representing the church, and the descriptions in verse 6 draw on various great stories of the Old Testament).

The Church, depicted by these two figures, follows in the footsteps of Jesus. They speak their message, and then evil destroys them: they are killed 'where also their Lord was crucified' (v. 8). The true Church 'takes up its cross' and follows its Lord. Then John sees them finally vindicated (vv. 11–12). So far, one might conclude that God's secret plan consists of the Church speaking and living as disciples in the world, through suffering and death, but eventually being vindicated. But what good is that?

Verse 13 is crucial. 'A tenth' of the city collapses; seven thousand people die. Both of these figures are reversals of Old Testament expectations (see Amos 5:3; 1 Kings 19:14–18), in which the *remnant* is said to be only a tenth, or only 7000 people. The rest 'give glory to God'—an expression always used to signify repentance. Judgment and power from heaven (chs. 6—9) did not bring about the repentance of the nations. But then comes this interlude (notice how, in verses 15–19, the judgments begin again, for 'the time' has come, v. 18), and in the interlude we see a depiction of the witness of the Church, resulting in salvation for many. Indeed, expectations are exceeded: it is not ten per cent who are saved but only ten per cent who are not.

We must remember again that what John sees sequentially does not refer to sequential events, as if the Church will witness at only one point in history. Rather, John presents us with two different futures. Judgment and power from heaven will not result in the nations returning to God, but the lived-out witness of the Church can achieve that result. The 'mystery of God' (10:7) is the witness of the Church, following the example of its Lord. It is this that can bring hope to the nations. This is an awesome responsibility.

Guidelines

This week's readings have been a heady mixture of bold imagery and gruesome visions. Out of them three themes emerge, which are worth pondering. First, there is the idea that God's servants are protected within our world but not protected from it. Indeed, the 'two messengers' in chapter 11 die as a result of their witness. We saw last week how deception, not persecution, was the key threat to the churches. It is difficult to hold together the idea that suffering and difficulty are part of our lives as we serve God, with the wider truth that God does protect and care for his servants.

We have also seen played out, in the visions, the point that power and force do not change people. In John's visions he saw that all God's power would not make people repent: the only hope was in the church's enfleshed proclamation about its Lord who died for others. This insight needs to affect our lives and our churches.

Finally, we were faced with the enormous and rather frightening idea that the difference between a positive and a negative future, between the nations' wailing being 'repentance' or 'too late', lies in the Church's role. It is the Church's witness that is the 'mystery of God'. Revelation is not black and white, as many suppose. Instead it holds out ambiguity and, with that, a challenge. All is not determined, and what will make the difference between hope and despair is whether the Church—that is, whether you and I—live out the example of Jesus.

How do you and your local church respond to this challenge?

FURTHER READING

Ian Boxall, *Revelation: Vision and Insight*, SPCK, 2002.

Christopher Rowland, *Revelation* (Epworth Commentary Series), Epworth Press, 1993.

Ben Wetherington, *Revelation* (New Cambridge Bible Commentary Series), Cambridge University Press, 2003.

Richard Bauckham, *The Theology of the Book of Revelation*, Cambridge University Press, 1993.

The BRF

Magazine

Richard Fisher writes...

BRF has three core ministries—prayer and spirituality, discipleship and Bible reading—which together reflect our statement of purpose: 'resourcing your spiritual journey'. We've decided now to take each of our core ministries in turn as the theme for *The BRF Magazine*. So, in this issue we explore prayer and spirituality, in May we'll look at discipleship, and in September Bible reading. BRF is about so much more than just Bible reading notes!

Spirituality: the spiritual search; the search for meaning and fulfilment; the sense that 'there must be more to life than this...' All around us, both within the church and beyond, people are searching to make sense of their lives. Most people recognize that there is a spiritual dimension to our being. One of the fastest-growing sectors of secular bookshops is 'Mind, Body, Spirit' where you will find a plethora of books expounding and promoting a bewildering range of spiritualities, remedies and new age solutions to 'life, the universe, and everything'.

At BRF we're trying to help people who are searching for a deeper spirituality. We're concerned that those who are seeking should encounter Christian spirituality, rather than any of the weird and wonderful alternatives. We're concerned to help Christians who want to go further and deeper in their relationship with God. We're

concerned to 'minister to the ministers'—to support and resource church leaders and teachers for their own spirituality, when they are giving out so much of themselves in their ministry. 'Lord, teach us to pray,' said the disciples to Jesus. Another aspect of our ministry here at BRF is to provide resources to help people to explore different aspects of and approaches to prayer. After all, most of us need help with our prayer lives.

And so in the following pages we reflect something of BRF's core ministry of prayer and spirituality. We hope that you enjoy this new approach to *The BRF Magazine* and that you will find your own thinking and reflection stimulated and challenged.

Richard Fisher, Chief Executive

Quiet Spaces: exploring prayer and spirituality

In 2005 BRF launched a new spirituality journal, to be published in March, July and November each year. *Quiet Spaces*, with its 'dip-in' collection of articles, poems, meditations and prayers, offers access to a wealth of material from a range of Christian traditions, to enrich your walk with God and help you live out your faith in everyday life. Each issue focuses on a single theme, the first three volumes covering 'Creation and creativity', 'The journey' and 'The feast'. The next issue, available from March 2006, will be devoted to 'The garden'. The extract below is taken from *Quiet Spaces: The Journey* and is written by Julie Watson, who, in March 2004, joined a trek through the Sinai desert.

The desert speaks

Welcome, travellers, welcome. Welcome to my world, for I am the desert in which you walk, following in the footsteps of thousands —seekers, pilgrims, runaways. However you arrived here, welcome.

I am old and shaped by wind and water, silent, empty and barren. I am the place that few seek, yet many find; for those who are driven to journey here are unaware that in the silence their own souls will shout more loudly. I have watched many journey across rock and sand, and seen their joy and tears. None can be unaffected by their time here, whether alone or with friends; each is silenced by the awesome power of the empti-ness or perhaps simply by the absence of their usual busy world.

Let me share with you some of my memories as I have watched the passing of time.

Long, long ago, a whole people passed through this desert—the children of Israel, a whole mass of humanity wandering after their God. Eventually they left the desert and entered their own land. Many years later I overheard another group: travelling from the east, they watched the night skies, seeking a special star that signified the birth of a great king. Soon after these magi, a young couple and their tiny baby passed through to hide in Egypt for a time, escaping a massacre, and when it was safe they returned home. Many have come over the years by choice or compulsion, journeying for a few days or weeks, months or even years, learning the wisdom of the desert.

Today another group has entered the land. They are eager and keen to explore, but how will they manage as the desert begins to explore each one of them? They begin at speed but soon slow down as solid rock turns to soft, flowing sand—two steps forward and one slide back. Faced by a huge sand dune, some are overwhelmed. Tantrum Hill, it has been named by those who wrestled with themselves to complete the challenge, for there is no way forward except to climb the dune; and even in a group, each person faces it alone. Some approach with quiet determination, others with tears and tantrums. They climb, finding that when they reach what appeared to be the top, another dune awaits. Time slows as they crawl ahead, then stand speechless at the top, for it is only there that the beauty of my presence is revealed and they clearly see the brown barren ground and the bright blue of the sky. For here there is no vegetation to mask the underlying rock and so the desert brings each one to face themselves and who they really are. Only now can they begin to understand the struggle and purpose of this journey.

Watching them descend slowly once again from the high peaks to the dry valleys, I wonder whether they will settle tonight. The thoughts that they have had will roll around in their minds, and sleep will be hard to find. The ground is hard too: lumps of granite protrude through the thin mattresses that they are trying to sleep on. In their sleeplessness, perhaps they will look up to the heavens around them and see the wonders encapsulated in the desert skies. For in the deep darkness stars have appeared, as if a child has sprinkled silver glitter over a huge expanse of thick black velvet. So many can be seen tonight that they are amazed, yet those stars have been above them every night of their lives. Before, they were in places filled with light, with comfortable beds and pleasant dreams; but now, in the deepest desert, the night reveals the beauty of the star-lit darkness. They will remember this night, and that hidden things are as real as those that can be seen and known.

Weary, they wake, wondering

Many pass through the desert without leaving footprints, for their journey is deep within themselves who chose for them to come this way, facing another day of walking —today down a wadi, a dry riverbed. After a time they will think that they have seen enough of sand and rock and that the desert is truly barren; then they will be surprised by flowers blossoming where they are least expected. Even in the deepest desert there is life, not as obvious as in their other world, for here water is scarce and hidden underground, a treasure of more value than gold. Plants and trees grow, their roots seeking a suggestion of water, growing towards the place that will give them life, deeper and deeper, building strong foundations for growth, reaching up to the sunshine and the highest heavens. Here the trees provide rest for weary travellers, a small pool of shade from the burning sun, an oasis of peace in the challenge of the journey.

Soon they will enter my gallery —sculptures made from sandstone, eroded by wind and water day by day cutting through sand that became stone, to return it to sand again and so complete the cycle. They have walked through the desert being surprised by awesome views, becoming aware of their weaknesses and the strength of their endurance; they have huddled into corners and tried to hide behind rocks; they have stood on the highest peaks and rejoiced in their own being. Soon they will leave the desert and be confronted once again by colour and noise and the busyness of the life they left behind, but they will never be the same again, for they have passed through the furnace of the desert and have been changed for ever.

Many pass through the desert without leaving footprints, for their journey is deep within themselves. Many fear finding the darkest night of the desert. But do not be afraid, my travellers, for I welcome you; and if you dare to embrace the desert, you will find riches beyond your wildest dreams.

Julie Watson is a minister in secular employment, working full-time as a Principal Lecturer at the University of Teesside and serving as Assistant Curate in Redcar.

Commendation for *Quiet Spaces* from The Revd Canon David Adam:

What a joy to have Quiet Spaces *and its offer of ways of journeying into the awareness of the Power, Peace and Presence of God… Let those who risk taking 'time out' to read* Quiet Spaces *be filled with the wonder, awe and beauty of what God presents to them each day.*

To order any of the Quiet Spaces *volumes or to subscribe regularly, please turn to the order forms on pages 158 and 159. You can also visit the website: www.quietspaces.org.uk.*

Michael Mitton

the
Rainbow
of renewal

FOREWORD BY DAVID RUNCORN

Daily Bible reflections for Lent and Easter

An extract from
The Rainbow of Renewal

This book of daily readings for Lent and Easter explores how the transforming power of God, through the work of the Holy Spirit, can bring renewal to each one of us. Different aspects of renewal are linked to colours of the rainbow, because rainbows are the essence of light. When the white light of God is projected through the prism of our lives, all the colours of renewal are revealed. The author is the Revd Michael Mitton, Project Officer for Renewing Ministry in the Derby Diocese. He has also written *A Heart to Listen* for BRF. The following extract is the reading for Ash Wednesday.

Exiles in Babylon

By the rivers of Babylon—there we sat down and there we wept when we remembered Zion. On the willows there we hung up our harps. For there our captors asked us for songs, and our tormentors asked for mirth, saying, 'Sing us one of the songs of Zion!' How could we sing the Lord's song in a foreign land? If I forget you, O Jerusalem, let my right hand wither! Let my tongue cling to the roof of my mouth, if I do not remember you, if I do not set Jerusalem above my highest joy. Remember, O Lord, against the Edomites the day of Jerusalem's fall, how they said, `Tear it down! Tear it down! Down to its foundations!' O daughter Babylon, you devastator! Happy shall they be who pay you back what you have done to us! Happy shall they be who take your little ones and dash them against the rock! (Psalm 137)

This psalm gives us an insight into a most devastating experience of corporate grief. When Joshua triumphantly marched the faithful people of God into the Promised Land, the future looked wonderful. God had rescued his people from Egypt; he had led them through the wilderness, and they then enjoyed an era of occupying the land that had been promised to them right at the beginning of their story of faith (Genesis 12:7). In time, God granted them their wish of having a king, and David was the one chosen for the task.

However, it was not long before David's descendants erred and strayed into just about every type of offence imaginable, and the kingdom became increasingly vulnerable to foreign invaders, as God withdrew his protection from the rebellious people. Eventually the unthinkable happened: a foreign people invaded Jerusalem; the mighty temple, which looked so indestructible, was pulled down; the king was blinded and led pathetically to imprisonment, and much of the population was marched ignominiously out of the city on another desert walk, this time not to the Holy Land, but away from it to Babylon.

So it was that they found themselves as refugees in a foreign land, where nothing was familiar, their faith was disregarded, and they were treated like slaves. Worst of all, God seemed to have abandoned them. They had believed he would preserve Jerusalem no matter what, and yet when it came to the crunch, he was apparently nowhere to be seen.

Thus, a group of them find themselves slumped down by the waters of Babylon, and all they can do is to think back to the good old days of Zion. Babylon was very different to Judea: it had an intricate system of canals, running across a huge, flat plain, which would have felt so different to the hills and valleys of Judea. They sit down by one of these canals and chat together, and one of them might say, 'Do you remember how at this time of year, we would go up to the temple to make our offering, go through that mighty gate and hear the sound of the busy market, and lis-

They found themselves refugees in a foreign land

ten to the prayers of the priest…' Others may join in, until it becomes too painful to continue. Each time they remember, they weep. It is what grieving people do. Those who have lost people they love want to recall many memories. We say, 'Do you remember how he used to…', 'Do you remember she loved to…', and it is a sort of bittersweet experience. We feel comforted by the remembrance, and yet it often brings tears, as we are aware of the extent of our loss.

The people of God in Babylon are no longer able to sing, and so they hang up their lyres. How painful it must have been when the captors taunted them, saying, 'Go on, sing us one of those odd songs you used to sing back in Jerusalem.' These were songs full of meaning and emotion for the Judeans, but for the Babylonians they were a source of mockery.

But the psalm tells us that these people of God, though deeply grieving, had an impressive stubbornness. Their inability to sing in a strange land does not mean they will forget Jerusalem—far from it. They may not understand, but they will hang on to hope. They'd sooner lose their hands and their tongues than forget Jerusalem. The psalm ends with terrible words that we find almost impossible to read—the vengeful killing of innocent children makes us think of callous terrorist blasts that are all too familiar in our day. There is deep hatred of the perpetrators of exile here, and the mourners give themselves strength in the only way they know how, which is to spit out venomous threats at their captors.

I have no idea what it must be like to be led away from a home and people I love and be taken to a land where all the customs and cultures are quite alien to me, where I cannot communicate because I don't know the language, and the people amongst whom I live view me with suspicion and distaste. I am all too aware that in this often sad and violent world that experience is far too common, and the issue of asylum seekers in 21st-century Britain is alerting us to the problems and pains of refugees. But for most of us this kind of exile is not something we are likely to experience personally. Nonetheless, it is quite possible to know a very deep sense of corporate loss at a way of life that once we took for granted, but now seems a million miles away.

The film adaptation of the first book of *The Lord of the Rings* begins with a mysterious voice narrating the words: 'The world has changed. I feel it in the water; I feel it in the earth; I smell it in the air. Much that once was is lost, for none now live who remember it.' The rest of the dramatic story builds upon the fact that things have taken place that have deeply disturbed the world, and no one really understands or remembers how it was, or how we got to this point. There are many in our churches who may feel this way: 'The church has changed… much that once was is lost.' There are people in the church where I serve who have been part of the congregation all their lives. They are in their 70s and 80s, and they have seen many different phases in the life of the church. They readily look back at the days when the building was full, the choir-stalls full of enthusiastic choristers of all ages, the Sunday School thriving, and the takings at the parish bazaar enough to cover the church costs. Now they look round at a society that has all but turned its back on God; they see that few churches have their own clergy, but have to share them with other churches; they witness clergy ignoring so many of the traditions that were once hallowed. Much that once was is lost. By the waters of the 21st-century post-modern, texting, Big-Brother-watching, eBay-shopping world, they sit down and weep.

Of course, it is not just the elderly who have this experience. Any of us can drive around this land and see once large churches in urban and rural situations now struggling with dwindling congregations, battling with the ever-increasing financial burdens of leaking roofs and crumbling walls, and we too can find ourselves thinking back to the good old days when churches looked very successful. We too can feel the dull ache of despair afflicting our souls.

And yet, paradoxically, this experience can be the beginning of renewal. For the people described in the psalm, their response was anger against the perpetrators of the humiliation and destruction that they had suffered. Today, in our longing for renewal, we can also easily end up with a 'blame' mentality, so that we look for those whom we can hold responsible for getting us into this situation. Others during that time of exile would have just shrugged their shoulders and said in effect, 'Oh well, this is now how it is. Let's settle down here in Babylon.' But thankfully there were prophets around who gave an inspiring lead to help people move from despair to hope and, in time, to make a journey of renewal to build a new Jerusalem. We shall look at this a bit more tomorrow, but today's task is to acknowledge how we feel about the losses that we have experienced individually and corporately in connection with the life of the church. You may be part of a church that once was alive in many ways, but now things have gone quiet and dry; you may once have belonged to a church that seemed so alive, but where you are now feels as if it lacks life by comparison; you may have left your church because you were disappointed with it, and now you live your Christian life more or less alone. Or maybe it is not your personal experience that bothers you, but you have a sense of connection with the wider community of the Church, and you grieve because in some areas of its life it has experienced many losses. If, on the other hand, you are in a church that is ablaze with renewal, then give thanks to God (and say a prayer for those who envy what you have).

Reflection

Think about your church situation—is it one of renewal at the moment? If it is, where do you see the renewal expressing itself? If not, what are your feelings about its situation? What is in your heart as you reflect on this? Grief? Blaming? Reluctant acceptance? Longing for the old days? Hope? You might like to try writing a psalm to express your feelings, making it your prayer to God.

Prayer

Lord, today is the beginning of Lent, and I choose to journey with you in these coming days. Only you know where you will lead me. Give me all that I need to let go of all that would weigh me down, and to be open to the new things you want to show me. Lead me by the waters of renewal.

To order a copy of this book, please turn to the order form on page 159.

Holy travelling

Deborah and David Douglas

When people went on pilgrimage in the Middle Ages, it was usually a matter of penance and indulgences: journeys to distant shrines might procure a saint's favour or subtract years from Purgatory. The renewed interest in pilgrimage among Christians of all denominations, however, has more to do with deepening a sense of the real presence of God in our lives. Contemporary pilgrimage, as the Anglican writer Evelyn Underhill once noted of spiritual retreat, 'puts in the foreground and keeps in the foreground that which is, after all, the first interest of religion: the soul's relation to God'.

Pilgrims, unlike tourists, tend to travel light. They have sloughed off daily distractions in exchange for prayerful attentiveness. Jesus promised his disciples that 'the Holy Spirit will bring to your remembrance all that I have said to you', and holy travelling often provides the ground for holy recollection.

On the map of Christianity, some places seem to draw visitors more powerfully than others. Scotland's Isle of Iona, for George MacLeod and others, has proved a 'thin place—only a tissue paper separating earth from heaven'. Such 'thin places', by means of their landscape, architecture, history and even weather, can evoke in travellers a sense of expectancy and clarity, and help to mediate the presence and grace of God. Just as there have been particularly credi-ble evangelists down the centuries, it's not surprising that there exist particularly credible witnesses of place.

But, at the same time, contemporary pilgrims keep in mind Evelyn Underhill's observation that 'from our human point of view some places are a great deal thinner than others: but to the eyes of worship the whole of the visible world, even its most unlikely patches, is rather "thin"'. Indeed, as Elizabeth Barrett Browning noted, 'Earth's crammed with heaven / And every common bush afire with God'.

Moreover, what draws pilgrims closer to God is not only the physical destination, but the people associated with it. In our own travels across Britain, as we researched and wrote our book, *Pilgrims in the Kingdom*, we discovered that what began with places led inexorably to the brave, visionary, joyful people who lived there—some in hermit caves and windswept islands, others in medieval monasteries or Victorian towns. We found that one of the great and unexpected gifts of pilgrimage was this expanded sense of the communion of saints.

Britain is uniquely rich in places to meet these heroes of the Christian faith. Both across time—from fourth-century mission centres to Coventry Cathedral's 21st-century ministry of reconciliation—and across Celtic, Catholic, Anglican and Protestant traditions, there are few better lands in the world, these two grateful Americans believe, to experience the wealth of Christendom's people and places.

Our years of exploration allowed us to sojourn in the landscape of Saint Ninian at Whithorn, and Saints Aidan and Cuthbert at Lindisfarne, and to glimpse the martyrdom sites of Thomas Becket in Canterbury and Margaret Clitherow in York. We understood more clearly the acts of faith carried out with humility and courage by Queen Margaret of Scotland, Lady Julian of Norwich and Nicholas Ferrar of Little Gidding.

We included in our book not only renowned pilgrimage destinations, but less traditional sites—such as John Wesley's Aldersgate Street (where he had 'felt his heart strangely warmed'), George Fox's Pendle Hill, and Evelyn Underhill's retreat house at Pleshey, where men

and women had directly experienced God's love and conveyed that possibility to others. We were immeasurably enriched as a result of travelling in the footsteps of such writers of faith as George Herbert in Bemerton, John Newton in Olney, Gerard Manley Hopkins at St Bueno's, and C.S. Lewis in Oxford.

T.S. Eliot honoured the chapel at Little Gidding as a place 'where prayer has been valid'. As we knelt there and in similar settings, we discovered that these journeys had led less to a gathering of historical information or a satisfaction of curiosity than to a strengthening of our lives in God.

For us, learning to pay attention in these places helped us to pay attention everywhere, to put ourselves daily in landscapes where we remain oriented towards God. We have found ourselves, in significant times of decision, thinking of these fellow pilgrims, remembering their faith and hope, and being fortified by their witness.

We can, by grace, return from pilgrimage sites with a heart open to the people who prayed there and to the God to whom they prayed—a possibility of transformation so profound as to be sacramental. When one has knelt where prayer has been valid, one rarely rises again quite the same.

Pilgrims in the Kingdom *was published by BRF in 2004. To order a copy, please turn to the order form on page 159.*

BRF's Prayer and Spirituality range

Naomi Starkey

As part of BRF's aim of resourcing people on their spiritual journey, no matter what stage they may be at, we publish a range of books that take as their focus different aspects of prayer and spirituality. These books complement our Bible reading notes and *Quiet Spaces* journal, by taking a more in-depth and systematic look at a whole range of themes to do with our relationship with God.

Interest in the general area of 'spirituality' has grown enormously over recent years, with many people aware of the importance of refreshing the soul as well as exercising the body. They are often equally aware of how hard it can be to do either, in the busyness of modern life. In building our Prayer and Spirituality range, we want to help people develop a Christian spirituality that is rooted in the Bible, watered by the Holy Spirit and nourished by fellowship with other believers.

Our books are divided into three main categories, to make it easier to identify which title would be most helpful for a particular need or situation. The categories are teaching about prayer; ways of praying; spiritual reading.

In our 'teaching about prayer' category, we include books that give helpful advice, often drawn from the author's own experience, about how to pray, even if you have never tried it before. *Long Wandering Prayer* by David Hansen is just such a book. It shows how prayer can take place just as easily on a long walk (and sometimes more so) as kneeling or sitting behind a closed door or even in a church. The author encourages us to let go of the drive to control our thoughts and offers advice on how to practise simply *being* in the presence of the living God.

In this same category, *Seeking God's Face* by Beryl Adamsbaum is a short and accessible little book that considers in straightforward terms why prayer is important, how to pray and stay grounded in scripture, how to grow in confidence as we approach and communicate with God, and what to do when God seems silent. A new study guide to accompany this book can be found on the BRF website.

Our 'ways of praying' category provides helpful material that can provide a way of getting started (or going deeper) in prayer. John Henstridge's *Transforming the Ordinary* offers a series of prayer meditations based around Bible passages that can transform the routines of daily life into moments to tune into God's presence. The meditations can be used by individuals and also in a group setting, and the book's introduction suggests ways of doing this.

A World of Prayer takes a different approach, presenting a globe-spanning collection of material that can be used for prayer and praise. It is compiled from the liturgies specially written for the annual services of Women's World Day of Prayer. Representing ten countries from Guatemala to Indonesia, the book includes worship material on a range of themes, such as caring for our world, healing and wholeness, and responding to God's call.

In our 'spiritual reading' category, we branch out from the act of praying itself, to considering how we relate to God both as individuals and as church communities, including how we can draw encouragement from less familiar parts of the Church as well as inspiring figures from Christian history. These are books designed to help people grow in faith through various life experiences, which celebrate the life and worship of the Church, and which offer essential fuel for the journey of discipleship.

The Flame of Sacred Love has been a popular title in this category for a number of years, selling nearly 6,000 copies to date. Written by the late Brother Ramon, a Franciscan hermit, it is an ideal introduction to the practice of contemplative prayer. Based around themes from the popular Charles Wesley hymn 'O thou who camest from above', it explores spiritual riches from across the Christian spiritual traditions—Orthodox, Catholic and Anglican. As well as teaching about spirituality, it also includes helpful prayer exercises that will provoke thought and stimulate the mind and heart to growth.

Taking the 'life experiences' theme, Wendy Bray's *In the Palm of God's Hand* is based on her personal prayer diary, written as she struggled with severe, long-term illness. Winner of the 2002 Biography of the Year at the Christian Book Awards, Wendy Bray's honest, moving and, incredibly, often funny account shows how personal faith can transform even the hardest of times and that God's love and mercy can still break through, no matter how tough the situation.

These are, of course, just a selection from the full Prayer and Spirituality range. To find out more about these books, and about the others we publish in this area, do visit our website: www.brf.org.uk.

Sounding the retreat

Martyn Payne

So, you're from *Barnabas* too. You know, Lucy was *so* good last year!' This is not the first time I have been greeted with words like these on my travels. I just have to hope I can somehow follow in my colleague's glorious footsteps.

The occasion was the Chichester Diocesan Children's Leaders' annual retreat, deep in the Sussex countryside near Lewes. A number of the leaders were regular attendees, who really look forward to this break from routine, which includes some beautiful countryside walks, plenty of time to relax and chat, sessions exploring God's word together and worship.

Our Friday evening to Sunday afternoon experience fell within the ten days between Ascension and Pentecost. For the followers of Jesus in that upper room, this was a time of waiting, praying and getting ready for the next stage of their work. It was easy, therefore, for us to be there in our imaginations and join the 120 that gathered at different times and who must have shared their stories and experiences of Jesus' ministry with each other.

We stepped in among those storytellers in Jerusalem and looked again at some of the incidents in John's Gospel in particular. We followed the beloved disciple's own prologue by trying to make sure that the 'Word became flesh' for us, so that we could fall in love with the story afresh. How else will we be able to share and be good news to the children we work with?

The tone of the sessions was conversational and reflective, using symbols and some *Godly Play* style presentations. All this, along with the powerful worship, splendid meals, fun and games, walks and plenty of laughter, played a vital part in restoring our souls.

This ministry really is an important but often neglected piece of the spiritual diet for those who work week-by-week faithfully and creatively with children. I would strongly recommend that churches consider Quiet Days or retreats as a way of resourcing their children's leaders. If you are interested in organizing one with *Barnabas*, then please be in touch. Sounding the retreat is certainly the way forward!

To support BRF's ministry with children, please see the form on page 156.

Children's spirituality

Kathryn Copsey

One of my most memorable encounters with children took place one Sunday afternoon in a church on an outer urban estate. A small group of about 30 of us were meeting for a regular Sunday afternoon service. The theme for the Sunday was Jesus' attitude to children: 'Unless you change and become like children you will never enter the kingdom of heaven.' Suddenly there was a scraping and scrabbling at the back of the church. The door flew open and the peace of the service was shattered by two boys of about nine or ten skimming up the side aisle of the church on rollerblades!

'Hello,' said the minister. 'Here, have a seat. You're just in time to help me with my talk.' He drew the giggling, half-embarrassed boys into the welcoming arms of the circle of people, and carried on. Then it was time for the prayers. Who said it was best to pray with your eyes shut? 'Psst,' said my neighbour. 'Better get those boys to empty their pockets.' While we'd been praying, they had helped themselves to the votive candle money sitting temptingly near. You had to admire their timing!

I must be honest: there was a sinking feeling in the pit of my stomach. We were a fragile group of people, some with mental health needs, others with learning disabilities. The last thing we needed were two lively boys making mischief. But the welcome and understanding offered by the others in the group (people who had no agenda about power and being 'adult', but identified with the marginal status of the children) made me realize yet again how we need constantly to allow Jesus' attitude to children to touch us and his words to transform us.

> *We need constantly to allow Jesus' attitude to children to touch us*

I wrote *From the Ground Up* (BRF, 2005) to share a little of my journey alongside children, to invite others to catch a glimpse of their rich spiritual world, and to share the thinking underlying CURBS (Children in URBan Situations), the charity that I have the privilege of leading. It is written against the background of a society that, with the intention of raising levels of 'success', is squeezing space for reflection, for nurturing a sense of awe and wonder, for music and art, for simple 'time to be', out of the curriculum. It is written at a time when 'yobs' are demonized, curfews are imposed, ASBOs are served on ever younger children, and the rise in under-16 pregnancies is a cause for concern. It is written when 'spirituality' is a buzz word featuring in the National Curriculum, yet in practice seems to be little understood. These are the experiences of many of the children we touch through CURBS.

The challenge for me is two-fold:

* What new perspectives on the child do I glean from the Bible?
* What new truths about myself, about the child and about society can I learn from the child?

I am totally convinced that if we take this challenge seriously, recognizing the key importance of the child's early years, we will learn how to restore children's damaged spirituality. In doing this we will offer them a pattern for life that will run counter to the image society has accorded them—which some of them have earned!

I have worked with children who have no sense of their own self-worth, attach no value to their thoughts and ideas, do not trust their feelings, have no opportunity to learn to make good choices, experience no trustworthiness or consistency from the adults in their lives, and have never learned to handle anger or hatred constructively. Yet Genesis 1:26 tells us that every single child we meet is made in God's image. Every single child has a spiritual dimension, a spirituality. God is present in *every* child we meet—even the most damaged. Do we listen to the news about the yobs and think, 'God himself is there within that young person'?

In the chapters leading up to Matthew 18, the disciples were taken up with 'adult' issues to do with comfort, security, certainty, competitiveness and status. Jesus had obviously got his priorities wrong: he was teaching that he was on his way to die in Jerusalem. Into the middle of the disciples' arguments, Jesus places a child— probably just an ordinary child who would have been hovering

God is present in every child we meet— even the most damaged

around. Children I work with hover around: difficult kids, damaged kids, lonely kids, kids at a loose end. No doubt kids hovered around Jesus: children know when a grown-up has a child-friendly heart. They hovered around enjoying Jesus' company; they waited in anticipation to hear him speak or see what he would do; they were ready to run an errand; they were confident that Jesus would have time for them; unlike the disciples, they had no thought of being 'great', they simply lived in the moment.

If we take Genesis and Matthew seriously, our attitude to children must completely change. We will take it seriously that each child has an inborn spirituality and that, in welcoming the child, we welcome Christ. We will take it seriously that unless we change and become like children we will *not enter* the kingdom of heaven.

Within CURBS, we act on our conviction that each child is created in God's image, recognizing, however, that this image is damaged by the world in which we live—damaged both unintentionally and intentionally. We believe that we need to repair this damaged spirituality in order for it to become a springboard for faith. We repair spirituality by the attitudes we model as adults, by the nurturing environments we offer a child, by the activities we engage in with the child that allow for the exploration of choices, feelings, wonder, emotions, trust and communication. Above all, we offer ourselves to the children through forming quality relationships with them, believing that God created us to be in relationship with others and with himself.

From the Ground Up invites us to walk through our world led by a child, and it challenges us to be transformed by the lessons learned on this walk.

For more information about CURBS, visit www.curbsproject.org.uk or email info@curbsproject.org.uk.

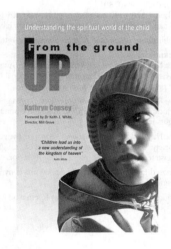

Kathryn Copsey is a trained community worker, and has worked with children for the past 30 years, mostly in urban situations such as East London. To order a copy of her book, From the Ground Up, *please turn to the order form on page 159.*

Guidelines © BRF 2006

The Bible Reading Fellowship
First Floor, Elsfield Hall, 15–17 Elsfield Way, Oxford OX2 8FG
Tel: 01865 319700; Fax: 01865 319701
E-mail: enquiries@brf.org.uk
Website: www.brf.org.uk

ISBN 1 84101 276 9

Distributed in Australia by:
Willow Connection, PO Box 288, Brookvale, NSW 2100.
Tel: 02 9948 3957; Fax: 02 9948 8153;
E-mail: info@willowconnection.com.au
Available also from all good Christian bookshops in Australia.
For individual and group subscriptions in Australia:
Mrs Rosemary Morrall, PO Box W35, Wanniassa, ACT 2903.

Distributed in New Zealand by:
Scripture Union Wholesale, PO Box 760, Wellington
Tel: 04 385 0421; Fax: 04 384 3990; E-mail: suwholesale@clear.net.nz

Distributed in the USA by:
The Bible Reading Fellowship, PO Box 380, Winter Park,
Florida 32790-0380
Tel: 407 628 4330 or 800 749 4331; Fax: 407 647 2406;
E-mail: brf@biblereading.org; Website: www.biblereading.org

Publications distributed to more than 60 countries

Printed in Singapore by Craft Print International Ltd

BRF is a Christian charity committed to resourcing the spiritual journey of adults and children alike. For adults, BRF publishes Bible reading notes and books and offers an annual programme of quiet days and retreats. Under its children's imprint *Barnabas*, BRF publishes a wide range of books for those working with children under 11 in school, church and home. BRF's *Barnabas Ministry* team offers INSET sessions for primary teachers, training for children's leaders in church, quiet days, and a range of events to enable children themselves to engage with the Bible and its message.

We need your help if we are to make a real impact on the local church and community. In an increasingly secular world people need even more help with their Bible reading, their prayer and their discipleship. We can do something about this, but our resources are limited. With your help, if we all do a little, together we can make a huge difference.

How can you help?

- You could support BRF's ministry with a donation or standing order (using the response form overleaf).

- You could consider making a bequest to BRF in your will, and so give lasting support to our work. (We have a leaflet available with more information about this, which can be requested using the form over-leaf.)

- And, most important of all, you could support BRF with your prayers.

Whatever you can do or give, we thank you for your support.

BRF – resourcing your spiritual journey

BRF MINISTRY APPEAL RESPONSE FORM

Name _____

Address _____

_____ Postcode _____

Telephone _____ Email _____

(Please tick boxes as appropriate. Delete as applicable where marked *)

Gift Aid Declaration

☐ I am a UK taxpayer. I want BRF to treat as Gift Aid Donations all donations I make from 6 April 2000 until I notify you otherwise.

Signature _____ Date _____

☐ I would like to support BRF's adult/children's* ministry with a regular donation by standing order (please complete the Banker's Order below).

Standing Order – Banker's Order

To the Manager, Name of Bank/Building Society _____

Address _____

_____ Postcode _____

Sort Code _____ Account Name _____

Account No _____

Please pay Royal Bank of Scotland plc, London Drummonds Branch, 49 Charing Cross, London SW1A 2DX (Sort Code 16-00-38), for the account of BRF A/C No. 00774151

The sum of _____ pounds on ___ /___ /___ (insert date your standing order starts) and thereafter the same amount on the same day of each month until further notice.

Signature _____ Date _____

Single donation

☐ I enclose my cheque/credit card/Switch card details for a donation of £5 £10 £25 £50 £100 (other) £_____ to support BRF's adult/children's* ministry)

Credit/ Switch card no. ☐☐☐☐☐☐☐☐☐☐☐☐☐☐☐☐☐☐☐

Expires ☐☐ ☐☐   Issue no. of Switch card ☐☐☐

Signature _____ Date _____

(Where appropriate, on receipt of your donation, we will send you a Gift Aid form)

☐ Please send me information about making a bequest to BRF in my will.

Please detach and send this completed form to: Richard Fisher, BRF, First Floor, Elsfield Hall, 15–17 Elsfield Way, Oxford OX2 8FG. BRF is a Registered Charity (No.233280)

Please note our subscription rates 2006–2007. From the May 2006 issue, the new subscription rates will be:

Individual subscriptions covering 3 issues for under 5 copies, payable in advance (including postage and packing):

		UK	SURFACE	AIRMAIL
GUIDELINES each set of 3 p.a.		£12.00	£13.35	£15.60
GUIDELINES 3-year sub	i.e. 9 issues	£29.55	N/A	N/A

Group subscriptions covering 3 issues for 5 copies or more, sent to ONE address (post free):

GUIDELINES   £10.05   each set of 3 p.a.

Please note that the annual billing period for Group Subscriptions runs from 1 May to 30 April.

Copies of the notes may also be obtained from Christian bookshops:

GUIDELINES   £3.35 each copy

SUBSCRIPTIONS

❑ I would like to take out a subscription myself (complete your name and
   address details only once)
❑ I would like to give a gift subscription (please complete both name and
   address sections below)

Your name _____

Your address _____

_____ Postcode _____

Gift subscription name _____

Gift subscription address _____

_____ Postcode _____

Please send *Guidelines* beginning with the May / September 2006 / January
2007 issue: (delete as applicable)

(please tick box)	UK	SURFACE	AIR MAIL
GUIDELINES	❑ £12.00	❑ £13.35	❑ £15.60
GUIDELINES 3-year sub	❑ £29.55		

I would like to take out an annual subscription to *Quiet Spaces* beginning
with the next available issue:

(please tick box)	UK	SURFACE	AIR MAIL
QUIET SPACES	❑ £16.95	❑ £18.45	❑ £20.85

Please complete the payment details below and send your coupon, with
appropriate payment, to: **BRF, First Floor, Elsfield Hall, 15–17 Elsfield Way,
Oxford OX2 8FG.**

Total enclosed £ _____ (cheques should be made payable to 'BRF')

Payment by cheque ❑ postal order ❑ Visa ❑ Mastercard ❑ Switch ❑

Card number: ☐☐☐☐☐☐☐☐☐☐☐☐☐☐☐☐☐☐☐

Expiry date of card: ☐☐☐☐   Issue number (Switch): ☐☐☐☐

Signature (essential if paying by credit/Switch card) _____

❑ Please do not send me further information about BRF publications.

BRF resources are available from your local Christian bookshop. BRF is a Registered Charity

GL0106

BRF PUBLICATIONS ORDER FORM

Please ensure that you complete and send off both sides of this order form.

Please send me the following book(s):

		Quantity	Price	Total
436 2	The Rainbow of Renewal (M. Mitton)	_____	£7.99	_____
269 6	A Heart to Listen (M. Mitton)	_____	£7.99	_____
265 3	Pilgrims in the Kingdom (D. & D. Douglas)	_____	£12.99	_____
386 2	From the Ground Up (K. Copsey)	_____	£6.99	_____
455 9	The Story of Easter (C. Doyle)	_____	£6.99	_____
456 7	Open the Door (V. Howie)	_____	£6.99	_____
026 X	Long Wandering Prayer (D. Hansen)	_____	£6.99	_____
370 6	Seeking God's Face (B. Adamsbaum)	_____	£4.99	_____
316 1	Transforming the Ordinary (J. Henstridge)	_____	£6.99	_____
369 2	A World of Prayer (ed. N. Starkey)	_____	£6.99	_____
037 5	The Flame of Sacred Love (Brother Ramon)	_____	£7.99	_____
336 6	In the Palm of God's Hand (W. Bray)	_____	£6.99	_____
245 9	PBC: Hosea—Micah (P. Gooder)	_____	£8.99	_____
095 2	PBC: Joshua & Judges (S. Mathewson)	_____	£7.99	_____
046 4	PBC: Mark (D. France)	_____	£8.99	_____

Total cost of books £ _____

Postage and packing (see over) £ _____

TOTAL £ _____

See over for payment details. All prices are correct at time of going to press, are subject to the prevailing rate of VAT and may be subject to change without prior warning.

BRF resources are available from your local Christian bookshop. BRF is a Registered Charity

PAYMENT DETAILS

Please complete the payment details below and send with appropriate payment and completed order form to:

**BRF, First Floor, Elsfield Hall,
15–17 Elsfield Way, Oxford OX2 8FG**

Name _____

Address _____

_____

_____ Postcode _____

Telephone _____

Email _____

Total enclosed £ _____ (cheques should be made payable to 'BRF')

Payment by cheque ❑ postal order ❑ Visa ❑ Mastercard ❑ Switch ❑

Card number: ☐☐☐☐☐☐☐☐☐☐☐☐☐☐☐☐☐☐☐

Expiry date of card: ☐☐☐☐   Issue number (Switch): ☐☐☐☐

Signature (essential if paying by credit/Switch card)_____

ALTERNATIVE WAYS TO ORDER

Christian bookshops: All good Christian bookshops stock BRF publications. For your nearest stockist, please contact BRF.

POSTAGE AND PACKING CHARGES				
order value	UK	Europe	Surface	Air Mail
£7.00 & under	£1.25	£3.00	£3.50	£5.50
£7.01–£30.00	£2.25	£5.50	£6.50	£10.00
Over £30.00	free	prices on request		

Telephone: The BRF office is open between 09.15 and 17.30. To place your order, phone 01865 319700; fax 01865 319701.

Web: Visit www.brf.org.uk

❑ Please do not send me further information about BRF publications.

BRF is a Registered Charity

GL0106